TEST PREPARATION

GACE

Special Education
Mathematics and Science
Secrets Study Guide
Part 2 of 2

DEAR FUTURE EXAM SUCCESS STORY

First of all, **THANK YOU** for purchasing Mometrix study materials!

Second, congratulations! You are one of the few determined test-takers who are committed to doing whatever it takes to excel on your exam. **You have come to the right place.** We developed these study materials with one goal in mind: to deliver you the information you need in a format that's concise and easy to use.

In addition to optimizing your guide for the content of the test, we've outlined our recommended steps for breaking down the preparation process into small, attainable goals so you can make sure you stay on track.

We've also analyzed the entire test-taking process, identifying the most common pitfalls and showing how you can overcome them and be ready for any curveball the test throws you.

Standardized testing is one of the biggest obstacles on your road to success, which only increases the importance of doing well in the high-pressure, high-stakes environment of test day. Your results on this test could have a significant impact on your future, and this guide provides the information and practical advice to help you achieve your full potential on test day.

Your success is our success

We would love to hear from you! If you would like to share the story of your exam success or if you have any questions or comments in regard to our products, please contact us at **800-673-8175** or **support@mometrix.com**.

Thanks again for your business and we wish you continued success!

Sincerely,
The Mometrix Test Preparation Team

> Need more help? Check out our flashcards at:
> http://MometrixFlashcards.com/GACE

TABLE OF CONTENTS

Science

Physics

BASIC EQUATION FOR WORK

The equation for **work** (W) is fairly simple: $W = F \times d$, where F is the force exerted and d is the displacement of the object on which the force is exerted. For the simplest case, when the vectors of force and displacement have the same direction, the work done is equal to the product of the magnitudes of the force and displacement. If this is not the case, then the work may be calculated as $W = Fd \cos \theta$, where θ is the angle between the force and displacement vectors. If force and displacement have the same direction, then work is positive; if they are in opposite directions, however, work is negative; and if they are perpendicular, the work done by the force is zero.

For example, if a man pushes a block horizontally across a surface with a constant force of 10 N for a distance of 20 m, the work done by the man is 200 N-m or 200 J. If instead the block is sliding and the man tries to **slow its progress** by pushing against it, his work done is –200 J, since he is pushing in the direction opposite the motion. Also, if the man pushes vertically downward on the block while it slides, his work done is zero, since his force vector is perpendicular to the displacement vector of the block.

> **Review Video: Push and Pull Forces**
> Visit mometrix.com/academy and enter code: 104731

It is important to note in each of these cases that neither the mass of the block nor the elapsed time is considered when calculating the amount of work done by the man.

> **Review Video: Work**
> Visit mometrix.com/academy and enter code: 681834

POWER

Put simply, **power** is the **rate at which work is done**. Power, like work, is a scalar quantity. If we know the amount of work, W, that has been performed in a given amount of time, Δt, then we may find average power, $P_{avg} = W / \Delta t$. If we are instead looking for the instantaneous power, there are two possibilities. If the force on an object is constant, and the object is moving at a constant velocity, then the instantaneous power is the same as the average power. If either the force or the velocity is varying, the instantaneous power should be computed by the equation $P = Fv$, where F and v are the instantaneous force and velocity. This equation may also be used to compute average power if the force and velocity are constant. Power is typically expressed in joules per second, or watts.

SIMPLE MACHINES

Simple machines include the inclined plane, lever, wheel and axle, and pulley. These simple machines have no internal source of energy. More complex or compound machines can be formed from them. Simple machines provide a force known as a mechanical advantage and make it easier to accomplish a task. The inclined plane enables a force less than the object's weight to be used to push an object to a greater height. A lever enables a multiplication of force. The wheel and axle allows for movement with less resistance. Single or double pulleys allow for easier direction of force. The wedge and screw are forms of the inclined plane. A wedge turns a smaller force working

1

over a greater distance into a larger force. The screw is similar to an incline that is wrapped around a shaft.

Review Video: Simple Machines
Visit mometrix.com/academy and enter code: 950789

MECHANICAL ADVANTAGE

A certain amount of **work** is required to move an object. The amount cannot be reduced, but by changing the way the work is performed a **mechanical advantage** can be gained. A certain amount of work is required to raise an object to a given vertical height. By getting to a given height at an angle, the effort required is reduced, but the distance that must be traveled to reach a given height is increased. An example of this is walking up a hill. One may take a direct, shorter, but steeper route, or one may take a more meandering, longer route that requires less effort. Examples of wedges include doorstops, axes, plows, zippers, and can openers.

LEVERS

A **lever** consists of a bar or plank and a pivot point or fulcrum. Work is performed by the bar, which swings at the pivot point to redirect the force. There are three types of levers: first, second, and third class. Examples of a **first-class lever** include balances, see-saws, nail extractors, and scissors (which also use wedges). In a **second-class lever** the fulcrum is placed at one end of the bar and the work is performed at the other end. The weight or load to be moved is in between. The closer to the fulcrum the weight is, the easier it is to move. Force is increased, but the distance it is moved is decreased. Examples include pry bars, bottle openers, nutcrackers, and wheelbarrows. In a **third-class lever** the fulcrum is at one end and the positions of the weight and the location where the work is performed are reversed. Examples include fishing rods, hammers, and tweezers.

Review Video: Levers
Visit mometrix.com/academy and enter code: 103910

WHEEL AND AXLE

The center of a **wheel and axle** can be likened to a fulcrum on a rotating lever. As it turns, the wheel moves a greater distance than the axle, but with less force. Obvious examples of the wheel and axle are the wheels of a car, but this type of simple machine can also be used to exert a greater force. For instance, a person can turn the handles of a winch to exert a greater force at the turning axle to move an object. Other examples include steering wheels, wrenches, faucets, waterwheels, windmills, gears, and belts. **Gears** work together to change a force. The four basic types of gears are spur, rack and pinion, bevel, and worm gears. The larger gear turns slower than the smaller, but exerts a greater force. Gears at angles can be used to change the direction of forces.

Review Video: Wheel and Axle
Visit mometrix.com/academy and enter code: 574045

PULLEYS

A **single pulley** consists of a rope or line that is run around a wheel. This allows force to be directed in a downward motion to lift an object. This does not decrease the force required, just changes its direction. The load is moved the same distance as the rope pulling it. When a **combination pulley** is used, such as a double pulley, the weight is moved half the distance of the rope pulling it. In this way, the work effort is doubled. Pulleys are never 100% efficient because of friction. Examples of pulleys include cranes, chain hoists, block and tackles, and elevators.

KINETIC ENERGY

The **kinetic energy of an object** is that quality of its motion that can be related in a qualitative way to the amount of work performed on the object. Kinetic energy can be defined as $KE = \frac{mv^2}{2}$, in which m is the mass of an object and v is the magnitude of its velocity. Kinetic energy cannot be negative, since it depends on the square of velocity. Units for kinetic energy are the same as those for work: joules. Kinetic energy is a scalar quantity.

Changes in kinetic energy occur when a force does work on an object, such that the speed of the object is altered. This change in kinetic energy is equal to the amount of work that is done, and can be expressed as $W = KE_f - KE_i = \Delta KE$. This equation is commonly referred to as the work-kinetic energy theorem. If there are several different forces acting on the object, then W in this equation is simply the total work done by all the forces, or by the net force. This equation can be very helpful in solving some problems that would otherwise rely solely on Newton's laws of motion.

POTENTIAL ENERGY

Potential energy is the amount of energy that can be ascribed to a body or bodies based on configuration. There are a couple of different kinds of potential energy. **Gravitational potential energy** is the energy associated with the separation of bodies that are attracted to one another gravitationally. Any time you lift an object, you are increasing its gravitational potential energy. Gravitational potential energy can be found by the equation $PE = mgh$, where m is the mass of an object, g is the gravitational acceleration, and h is its height above a reference point, most often the ground.

Another kind of potential energy is **elastic potential energy**; elastic potential energy is associated with the compression or expansion of an elastic, or spring-like, object. Physicists will often refer to potential energy as being stored within a body, the implication being that it could emerge in the future.

> **Review Video: Potential and Kinetic Energy**
> Visit mometrix.com/academy and enter code: 491502

CONSERVATIVE AND NON-CONSERVATIVE FORCES

Forces that change the state of a system by changing kinetic energy into potential energy, or vice versa, are called **conservative forces**. This name arises because these forces conserve the **total amount of kinetic and potential energy**. Every other kind of force is considered non-conservative. One example of a conservative force is gravity. Consider the path of a ball thrown straight up into the air. Since the ball has the same amount of kinetic energy when it is thrown as it does when it returns to its original location (known as completing a closed path), gravity can be said to be a conservative force. More generally, a force can be said to be conservative if the work it does on an object through a closed path is zero. Frictional force would not meet this standard, of course, because it is only capable of performing negative work.

ONE-DIMENSIONAL ANALYSIS OF WORK DONE BY A VARIABLE FORCE

If the force on an object varies across the distance the object is moved, then a simple product will not yield the work. If we consider the work performed by a variable force in one dimension, then we are assuming that the directions of the force and the displacement are the same. The magnitude of the force will depend on the position of the particle. In order to calculate the amount of work performed by a variable force over a given distance, we should first divide the total displacement into a number of intervals, each with a width of Δx. We may then say that the amount of work performed during any one interval is $\Delta W = F_{avg}\Delta x$, where F_{avg} is the average force over the interval Δx. We can then say that the total amount of work performed is the sum of all work performed during the various intervals. By reducing the interval to an infinitesimal length, we obtain the integral:

$$W = \int_{x_1}^{x_2} F_x dx$$

This integral requires that the force be a known function of x.

WORK PERFORMED BY A SPRING

If we move a block attached to a spring from point x_i to point x_f, we are doing work on the block, and the spring is also doing work on the block. To determine the work done by the spring on the block, we can substitute F from Hooke's law into our equation for work performed by a variable force, and arrive at this measure: $W = \frac{k(x_i{}^2 - x_f{}^2)}{2}$. This work will be positive if $x_i{}^2 > x_f{}^2$, and negative if the opposite is true. If $x_i = 0$ and we decide to call the final position x, then we may change our equation: $W = \frac{-kx^2}{2}$. It is important to keep in mind that this is the work done by the spring. The work done by the force that moves the block to its final position will be a positive quantity.

Like all simple harmonic oscillators, springs operate by **storing and releasing potential energy**. The amount of energy being stored or released by a spring is equal to the magnitude of the work done by the spring during that same operation. The total potential energy stored in a spring can be calculated as $PE = \frac{kx^2}{2}$. Neglecting the effects of friction and drag, an object oscillating on a spring will continue to do so indefinitely, since total mechanical energy (kinetic and potential) is conserved. In such a situation, the period of oscillation can be calculated as $T = 2\pi \times \sqrt{\frac{m}{k}}$.

DISPLACEMENT

When something changes its location from one place to another, it is said to have undergone **displacement**. If we can determine the original and final position of the object, then we can determine the total displacement with this simple equation:

$$\Delta x = final\ position - original\ position$$

If the object has moved in the positive direction, then the final position will be greater than the original position, so we can say that the change was positive. If the final position is less than the original, however, displacement will be negative. Displacement along a straight line is a very simple example of a vector quantity; it has both a magnitude and a direction. If an object travels from position $x = -5$ cm to $x = 5$ cm, it has undergone a displacement of 10 cm. If it traverses the same path in the opposite direction, its displacement is –10 cm. A vector that spans the object's displacement in the direction of travel is known as a displacement vector, with units of length.

Review Video: <u>Displacement in Physics</u>
Visit mometrix.com/academy and enter code: 236197

DETERMINING POSITION

In order to determine anything about the **motion of an object**, we must first **locate it**. In other words, we must be able to describe its position relative to some reference point, often called an **origin**. If we consider the origin as the zero point of an axis, then the positive direction of the axis will be the direction in which measuring numbers are getting larger, and the negative direction is that in which the numbers are getting smaller. If a particle is located 5 cm from the origin in the positive direction of the x-axis, its location is said to be $x = 5$ cm. If another particle is 5 cm from the origin in the negative direction of the x-axis, its position is $x = -5$ cm. These two particles are 10 cm apart. A vector whose starting point is the origin and whose endpoint is the location of an object is that object's position vector, with units of length.

VELOCITY

INSTANTANEOUS VELOCITY

There are two types of velocity that are commonly considered in physics: **average velocity** and **instantaneous velocity**. In order to obtain the *instantaneous velocity* of an object, we must find its average velocity and then try to decrease Δt as close as possible to zero. As Δt decreases, it approaches what is known as a *limiting value*, bringing the average velocity very close to the instantaneous velocity. Instantaneous velocity is most easily discussed in the context of calculus-based physics.

AVERAGE VELOCITY

If we want to calculate the *average velocity* of an object, we must know two things. First, we must know its **displacement**, or the **distance** it has covered. Second, we must know the **time it took to cover this distance**. Once we have this information, the formula for average velocity is quite simple: $v_{avg} = \frac{(x_f - x_i)}{(t_f - t_i)}$, where the subscripts i and f denote the initial and final values of the position and time. In other words, the average velocity is equal to the change in position divided by the change in time. This calculation will indicate the average distance that was covered per unit of time. **Average velocity is a vector** and will always point in the same direction as the displacement vector (since time is a scalar and always positive).

ACCELERATION

Acceleration is the **change in the velocity** of an object. Like velocity, acceleration may be computed as an average or an instantaneous quantity. To calculate average acceleration, we may use this simple equation: $a_{avg} = \frac{v_f - v_i}{t_f - t_i}$, where the subscripts i and f denote the initial and final values of the velocity and time. The so-called instantaneous acceleration of an object can be found by reducing the time component to the limiting value until instantaneous velocity is approached. Acceleration will be expressed in units of distance divided by time squared; for instance, meters per second squared. Like position and velocity, acceleration is a vector quantity and will therefore have both magnitude and direction.

Review Video: Velocity and Acceleration
Visit mometrix.com/academy and enter code: 671849

5

KINEMATICS

KINEMATIC EQUATIONS

The phenomenon of constant acceleration allows physicists to construct a number of helpful equations. Perhaps the most fundamental equation of an object's motion is the **position equation**:

$$x = x_i + v_i t + \frac{1}{2}at^2$$

If the object is starting from rest at the origin, this equation reduces to $x = \frac{at^2}{2}$. The position equation can be rearranged to give the **displacement equation**:

$$\Delta x = v_i t + \frac{1}{2}at^2$$

If the object's acceleration is unknown, the position or displacement may be found by the equation:

$$\Delta x = \frac{(v_f + v_i)t}{2}$$

If the position of an object is unknown, the velocity may be found by the equation:

$$v = v_i + at$$

Similarly, if the time is unknown, the velocity after a given displacement may be found by the equation:

$$v = \sqrt{(v_i{}^2 + 2a\Delta x)}$$

PROJECTILE MOTION

When we discuss **projectile motion**, we are referring to the movement of an object through two dimensions during a free fall. Two-dimensional motion may be described using the same equations as one-dimensional motion, but two equations must be considered simultaneously. For basic equations for projectile motion, it is often assumed that the rate of gravitational acceleration on the earth is $g = 9.8$ m/s^2, and that the effect of air resistance can be ignored (Note: take care with the sign on gravitational acceleration make sure that it always points toward the earth). If a projectile is launched under such ideal conditions, we may say that its initial velocity is $v_0 = v_0 \cos\theta\, \mathbf{i} + v_0 \sin\theta\, \mathbf{j}$. These two velocity components are sometimes written as v_{0x} and v_{0y}, respectively.

Example: If a cannon located at a height of 5 m above ground level fires a cannonball 250 m/s at an angle of $\frac{\pi}{6}$ from the horizontal, how far will the cannonball travel before hitting the ground?

When the cannonball hits the ground, it has been displaced by -5 m in the y-direction. Solving for the components of initial velocity yields $v_{0x} = 216.5$ m/s and $v_{0y} = 125$ m/s. Setting up the y-direction displacement equation results in the following: $-5 = 125t_f - 4.9t_f{}^2$. Solving for t_f yields an impact time of around 25.5 seconds. To find the horizontal distance covered, simply set up the displacement equation for the x-direction: $\Delta x = v_{0x}t_f + \frac{1}{2}a_x(t_f)^2$. Since we ignore the effects of air resistance, acceleration in the x-direction is zero, yielding a flight distance of 5,530 m.

> **Review Video: Projectile Motion**
> Visit mometrix.com/academy and enter code: 719700

6

UNIFORM CIRCULAR MOTION

We may say that a particle is in **uniform circular motion** when it is traveling in a circle, or circular arc, and at a constant speed. Crucially, we must note that such a particle is accelerating, even though the magnitude of its velocity does not change. This is because velocity is a vector, and consequently, any change in its direction is an acceleration. So, if we take two points on an arc of radius, r, separated by an angle, θ, and want to determine the time it will take a particle to move between these two points at a constant speed, $|v|$, we can use the equation: $\Delta t = \frac{r\theta}{|v|}$. The quantity $\frac{|v|}{r}$ is often written as ω, or angular velocity, having units of radians per second, so the time may also be computed as $\Delta t = \frac{\theta}{\omega}$. The speed, or absolute value of the velocity, of an object in uniform circular motion is also called the tangential speed, because the object is always moving in a direction tangent to the circle. Similarly, an increase in the magnitude of this velocity is called **tangential acceleration**.

A very important component of uniform motion is the centripetal acceleration. This is the acceleration that changes the direction of the velocity vector to follow the circular arc. It is directed toward the center of the circle or arc and is described by $a_c = \frac{|v|^2}{r} = r\omega^2$.

RELATIVE MOTION AND INERTIAL REFERENCE FRAMES

When we describe motion as being **relative**, we mean that it can only be measured in relation to something else. If a moving object is considered as it relates to some stationary object or arbitrary location, it will have a different measured velocity than it would if it were compared to some other object that is itself in motion. In other words, the measure of an object's velocity depends entirely on the reference frame from which the measurement is taken. When performing measurements of this kind, we may use any reference point we like. However, once we have decided on a reference point, we must be consistent in using it as the basis for all of our measurements, or else we will go astray. Additionally, if we want to be able to apply Newton's laws of motion or Galilean principles of relativity, we must select an **inertial reference frame**: that is, a reference frame that is not accelerating or rotating. A car traveling at a constant speed in a straight line is an inertial reference frame. A car moving in uniform circular motion is not.

An object's velocity with respect to a frame fixed to the earth can be computed by measuring its velocity from any inertial reference frame and combining that velocity by vector addition with the velocity of the inertial frame with respect to the earth. For instance, if a man is traveling in the x-direction at 20 m/s, and he throws a rock out the window at a relative velocity of 15 m/s in the y-direction, the rock's velocity with respect to the earth is found by adding the two vectors:

$$v_r = 20\mathbf{i} + 15\mathbf{j} \text{ m/s}$$

NEWTON'S LAWS
NEWTON'S FIRST LAW

Before Newton formulated his laws of mechanics, it was generally assumed that some force had to act on an object continuously in order to make the object move at a **constant velocity**. Newton, however, determined that unless some other force acted on the object (most notably friction or air resistance), it would continue in the direction it was pushed at the same velocity forever. In this light, a body at rest and a body in motion are not all that different, and Newton's first law makes little distinction. It states that a body at rest will tend to remain at rest, while a body in motion will tend to remain in motion. This phenomenon is commonly referred to as **inertia**, the tendency of a body to remain in its present state of motion. In order for the body's state of motion to change, it must be acted on by a non-zero net force. **Net force** is the vector sum of all forces acting on a body. If this vector sum is zero, then there is no unbalanced force, and the body will remain in its present state of motion. It is important to remember that this law only holds in inertial reference frames.

> **Review Video: <u>Newton's First Law of Motion</u>**
> Visit mometrix.com/academy and enter code: 590367

NEWTON'S SECOND LAW

Newton's second law states that an **object's acceleration** is directly proportional to the net force acting on the object, and inversely proportional to the object's mass. It is generally written in equation form $F = ma$, where F is the net force acting on a body, m is the mass of the body, and a is its acceleration. It is important to note from this equation that since the mass is always a positive quantity, the acceleration vector is always pointed in the same direction as the net force vector. Of course, in order to apply this equation correctly, one must clearly identify the body to which it is being applied. Once this is done, we may say that F is the vector sum of all forces acting on that body, or the net force. This measure includes only those forces that are external to the body; any internal forces, in which one part of the body exerts force on another, are discounted. Newton's second law somewhat encapsulates his first, because it includes the principle that if no net force is acting on a body, the body will not accelerate. As was the case with his first law, Newton's second law may only be applied in inertial reference frames.

> **Review Video: <u>Newton's Second Law of Motion</u>**
> Visit mometrix.com/academy and enter code: 737975

NEWTON'S THIRD LAW

Newton's third law of motion is quite simple: **for every force, there is an equal and opposite force**. When a hammer strikes a nail, the nail hits the hammer just as hard. If we consider two objects, A and B, then we may express any contact between these two bodies with the equation $F_{AB} = -F_{BA}$. It is important to note in this kind of equation that the order of the subscripts denotes which body is exerting the force. Although the two forces are often referred to as the **action** and **reaction** forces, in physics there is really no such thing. There is no implication of cause and effect in the equation for Newton's third law. At first glance, this law might seem to forbid any movement at all. We must remember, however, that these equal, opposite forces are exerted on different bodies with different masses, so they will not cancel each other out.

> **Review Video: <u>Newton's Third Law of Motion</u>**
> Visit mometrix.com/academy and enter code: 838401

STATIC AND KINETIC FRICTIONAL FORCES

In order to illustrate the concept of friction, let us imagine a book resting on a table. As it sits there, the force of its **weight** (W) is equal and opposite to the **normal force** (N). If, however, we were to exert a force (F) on the book, attempting to push it to one side, a **frictional force** (f) would arise, equal and opposite to our force. This kind of frictional force is known as *static frictional force*. As we increase our force on the book, however, we will eventually cause it to accelerate in the direction of our force. At this point, the frictional force opposing us will be known as *kinetic frictional force*. For the most part, kinetic frictional force is lower than static frictional force, and so the amount of force needed to maintain the movement of the book will be less than that needed to initiate movement. For wheels and spherical objects on a surface, static friction at the point of contact allows them to roll, but there is a frictional force that resists the rolling motion as well, due primarily to

deformation effects in the rolling material. This is known as rolling friction, and tends to be much smaller than either static or kinetic friction.

Equilibrium

We may say that an object is in a **state of equilibrium** when it has a **constant linear momentum** P at its center of mass, and when **angular momentum L is also constant about the center of mass**. In other words, a wheel may be in equilibrium when it is spinning at a constant speed, and a hockey puck may be in equilibrium as it slides across ice. These are both examples of **dynamic equilibrium**. The phrase **static equilibrium**, however, is reserved for objects in which both linear and angular momentum are at zero. An object sitting on a table could be considered as being in static equilibrium.

Using Equilibrium Conditions

For a **body in equilibrium**, the net force vector and the net torque vector will both be equal to zero. For the most common cases, two-dimensional systems, these conditions can be fully expressed by one or two force summation equations and one torque summation equation. Torque summations may be taken about any point on the body, though strategic placement can make calculations simpler. To determine the **torque exerted by a force**, simply multiply the magnitude of the force by the perpendicular distance to the point of interest. It will be necessary to decide in advance which direction of torque (clockwise or counterclockwise) will be considered positive.

For example, if we have a bar of known mass, m, that is suspended by cables at each end and whose center of mass is two thirds of the way along its length, L, we can use the equilibrium conditions to determine the tension in each cable. Gravity exerts a force of $-mg$ on the bar's center of mass. Translational equilibrium conditions tell us that $T_1 + T_2 - mg = 0$. Setting the total torque about the center of mass equal to zero, considering counterclockwise torque to be positive, yields the equation $T_2\left(\frac{L}{3}\right) - T_1\left(\frac{2L}{3}\right) = 0$. Solving these equations results in $T_1 = \frac{mg}{3}$ and $T_2 = \frac{2mg}{3}$. This result makes sense since the center of mass is closer to the second cable.

Translational and Rotational Equilibrium

If a body is in **translational equilibrium**, then its linear momentum will be constant, and there will be a net force of zero. Likewise, a body in rotational equilibrium will have a constant angular momentum, and again there will be a net torque of zero. Both of these equations are vector equations, and as such are both equivalent to three scalar equations for the three dimensions of motion, though in most instances, only one or two dimensions will be considered at a time. We may say that the two requirements for a body to be in equilibrium are that the vector sum of all the external forces acting on the body must be zero, and the vector sum of all the external torques acting on the body must also be zero. Conversely, if we are told that a body is in equilibrium, we may assume that both of these conditions will hold, and that we can use them to find unknown forces or torques.

Friction

The **first property of friction** is that, if the body does not move when horizontal force F is applied, then the static frictional force is exactly equal and opposite to F. Static frictional force has a maximum value, however, which is expressed as $f_{s,max} = \mu_s N$, in which μ_s is the coefficient of static friction, and N is the magnitude of the normal force. If the magnitude of F should exceed the maximum value of static friction, the body will begin to move. Once the body has begun to slide, the frictional force will generally decrease. The value to which the frictional force will diminish is expressed as $f_k = \mu_k N$, in which μ_k is the coefficient of kinetic friction. For objects inclined to roll,

9

such as balls or wheels, there is a rolling frictional force that resists the continued rolling of such an object. This force is expressed by $f_r = \mu_r N$, in which μ_r is the coefficient of rolling friction. All of these frictional coefficients are dimensionless. Since the value of the frictional force depends on the interaction of the body and the surface, it is usually described as friction between the two.

APPLYING CONSERVATION OF ROTATIONAL ENERGY AND ANGULAR MOMENTUM

A metal hoop of mass m and radius r is released from rest at the top of a hill of height h. Assuming that it rolls without sliding and does not lose energy to friction or drag, what will be the hoop's angular and linear velocities upon reaching the bottom of the hill?

The hoop's initial energy is all potential energy, $PE = mgh$. As the hoop rolls down, all of its energy is converted to **translational** and **rotational kinetic energy**. Thus, $mgh = \frac{1}{2}mv^2 + \frac{1}{2}I\omega^2$. Since the moment for a hoop is $I = mr^2$, and $\omega = \frac{v}{r}$, the equation becomes $mgh = \frac{1}{2}mv^2 + \frac{1}{2}mr^2\left(\frac{v^2}{r^2}\right)$, which further simplifies to $gh = v^2$. Thus, the resulting velocity of the hoop is $v_f = \sqrt{gh}$, with an angular velocity of $\omega_f = \frac{v_f}{r}$. Note that if you were to forget about the energy converted to rotational motion, you would calculate a final velocity of $v_f = \sqrt{2gh}$, which is the **impact velocity** of an object dropped from height h.

Angular momentum, L, of an object is defined as its moment of inertia multiplied by its angular velocity, or $L = I\omega$. Consider a planet orbiting the sun with an elliptical orbit where the small radius is r_S and large radius is r_L. Find the angular velocity of the planet when it is at distance r_S from the sun if its velocity at r_L is ω_L.

Since the size of a planet is almost insignificant compared to the interplanetary distances, the planet may be treated as a single particle of mass m, giving it a moment about the sun of $I = mr^2$. Since the gravitational force is incapable of exerting a net torque on an object, we can assume that the planet's angular momentum about the sun is a constant, $L_L = L_S$. Thus, $mr_L^2\omega_L = mr_S^2\omega_S$. Solving this equation for ω_S yields $\omega_S = \omega_L\left(\frac{r_L}{r_S}\right)^2$.

MASS-ENERGY RELATIONSHIP

Because mass consists of atoms, which are themselves formed of subatomic particles, there is an energy inherent in the composition of all mass. If all the atoms in a given mass were formed from their most basic particles, it would require a significant input of energy. This rest energy is the energy that Einstein refers to in his famous mass-energy relation $E = mc^2$, where c is the speed of light in a vacuum. In theory, if all the subatomic particles in a given mass were to spontaneously split apart, it would give off energy $E = mc^2$. For example, if this were to happen to a single gram of mass, the resulting outburst of energy would be $E = 9 \times 10^{13}$ J, enough energy to heat more than 200,000 cubic meters of water from the freezing point to the boiling point.

In some nuclear reactions, small amounts of mass are converted to energy. The amount of energy released can be calculated through the same relation, $E = mc^2$. Most such reactions involve mass losses on the order of 10^{-30} kg.

WEIGHT

Too often, **weight** is confused with **mass**. Strictly speaking, weight is the force pulling a body towards the center of a nearby astronomical body. Of course, in the case of most day-to-day operations for human beings, that astronomical body is the earth. The reason for weight is primarily a gravitational attraction between the masses of the two bodies. The SI unit for weight is the Newton. In general, we will be concerned with situations in which bodies with mass are located where the free-fall acceleration is g. In these situations, we may say that the magnitude of the weight vector is $W = mg$. As a vector, weight can be expressed as either $-mg\mathbf{j}$ or $-W\mathbf{j}$, in which $\mathbf{j}$ is the direction on the axis pointing away from the earth.

> **Review Video: Mass, Weight, Volume, Density, and Specific Gravity**
> Visit mometrix.com/academy and enter code: 920570

COMMON MEANS OF TRANSFERRING ELECTRICAL CHARGE

Charge is transferred in three common ways: conduction, induction, and friction. **Conduction**, as the name implies, takes place between conductive materials. There must be a point of contact between the two materials and a potential difference, such as when a battery is connected to a circuit. **Induction** also requires conductive materials. It occurs due to one material encountering a varying magnetic field. This can be the result of a changing magnetic field or the material moving within a constant magnetic field. Charge transfer due to **friction** does not require conductive materials. When two materials are rubbed together, electrons may be transferred from one to the other, leaving the two materials with equal and opposite charges. This is observed when shoes are dragged across a carpeted floor.

> **Review Video: Charging by Conduction**
> Visit mometrix.com/academy and enter code: 502661

CONDUCTORS, INSULATORS, AND SEMICONDUCTORS

In many materials, electrons are able to move freely; these are known as **conductors**. Due to their atomic structure and delocalized electrons, **metals** tend to be the best conductors, particularly copper and silver. Highly conductive wires are instrumental in creating low-resistance pathways for electrons to travel along within a circuit.

Other materials naturally inhibit the movement of charge and are known as **insulators**. Their electrons are tightly held by the individual constituent atoms. Glass, pure water, wood, and plastic are all insulators. Insulators are necessary in circuits to prevent charge from escaping to undesirable places, such as an operator's hand. For this reason, most highly conductive materials are covered by insulators.

Semiconductors, as the name suggests, are materials that only partially conduct electrical charge. The elements silicon and germanium are both common semiconductors, and are frequently used in microelectronic devices because they allow for tight control of the rate of conduction. In many cases, the conduction ability of semiconductors can be controlled by adjusting the temperature of the material.

ELECTRIC CURRENT

An **electric current** is simply an **electric charge in motion**. Electric current cannot exist unless there is a difference in electric potential. If, for instance, we have an isolated conducting loop, it will be at the same potential throughout. If, however, we insert a battery into this loop, then the conducting loop will no longer be at a single electric potential. A flow of electrons will result and will very quickly reach a steady state. At that point, it will be completely analogous to steady-state fluid flow. A current is quantified by the amount of charge that is transferred in a given amount of time. The SI unit for current is the ampere (A), equal to a coulomb of charge per second.

> **Review Video: Electric Charge**
> Visit mometrix.com/academy and enter code: 323587

ELECTROMOTIVE FORCE AND COMMON EMF DEVICES

A force that maintains a potential difference between two locations in a circuit is known as an **electromotive force.** A device that creates this force is referred to as an EMF device. The most common EMF device is the battery. **Batteries** operate by converting chemical energy stored in the electrolyte, the internal chemical material, into electrical energy. The reaction causes a lack of electrons on the cathode, and when the circuit is connected, they flow from the anode, creating a flow of current. The electrolyte's composition also determines whether the battery is classified as acidic or alkaline, and wet or dry. Another EMF device is the **photocell**, also commonly called the solar cell, since most photocells are powered by the sun. These operate by absorbing photons, which cause the electrons to be excited and flow in a current, a process of converting light energy into electrical energy. A third type of EMF device is the **generator**. This device converts mechanical energy to electrical energy. A generator may be powered by such diverse sources as gasoline engines, flowing water, or even manually powered cranks. These devices utilize a rotating shaft to spin a coil within a magnetic field, creating a potential difference by induction.

OHM'S LAW

If we were to apply the exact same potential difference between the ends of two geometrically similar rods, one made of copper and one made of glass, we would create vastly different currents. This is because these two substances have different **resistances**. Ohm's Law describes the relation between applied voltage and induced current, $V = IR$. This is one of the most important tools of circuit analysis. Resistance, then, can be calculated as $R = \frac{V}{I}$. The SI unit for resistance is the **ohm** (Ω), equal to a volt per ampere. When a conductor is placed into a circuit to provide a specific resistance, it is known as a resistor. For a given potential difference, the greater the resistance is to the current, the smaller the current will be.

If we wish to look instead at the quality of the material of which the resistor is made, then we must consider resistivity. **Resistivity**, ρ, is a physical property of every material, which, if known, can be used to size a resistor for a specific resistance. Resistance is dictated by both the material and the dimensions of the resistor, given by the relation $R = \frac{\rho L}{A}$, where L is the effective length of the resistor and A is the effective cross-section. Alternatively, an unknown resistivity may be calculated by rearranging the equation as $\rho = \frac{RA}{L}$.

The resistivity will often change with temperature. In these cases, the relevant resistivity may be calculated $\rho = p_{ref}\left(1 + \alpha(T - T_{ref})\right)$, where α is the resistivity proportionality constant and T is the material temperature.

> **Review Video: Resistance of Electric Currents**
> Visit mometrix.com/academy and enter code: 668423

ENERGY AND POWER

Electric circuits operate by **transferring** electrical energy from one location in the circuit to another. Some devices in a circuit can store and release energy while other devices, like resistors, simply dissipate energy. **Power** is a measure of the rate at which energy is stored, released, transferred, or dissipated. It is measured in watts (W), or joules per second. Power is calculated by $P = VI$. The amount of power being released by a 9-V battery producing a current of 5 A is 45 W. When calculating the amount of power dissipated by a resistor, Ohm's Law allows two other equations for power, $P = I^2R = \frac{V^2}{R}$.

When power consumption over long periods of time needs to be measured, it will often be measured in units of kilowatt-hours, which is the amount of energy consumed at a rate of 1 kW over the course of an hour. One kilowatt-hour is equal to 3,600 kJ.

CAPACITORS AND DIELECTRICS

Capacitors are devices used in circuits to store energy in the form of electric fields. They are most often composed of two oppositely charged parallel plates separated by a medium, generally air. This medium is referred to as the capacitor's **dielectric**. The dielectric material dictates the amount of energy in the electric field and, consequently, the amount of energy that can be stored by the capacitor. The measurable quality of a capacitor is known as its **capacitance**, or the amount of charge that it can store per volt of potential difference. This is given by the equation $C = \frac{Q}{V}$, with capacitance having units of farads or coulombs per volt. Physically, the capacitance depends on three things: the **area** of the parallel plates, the **separation distance** between them, and the **dielectric** material. For cases in which the separation distance is insignificant compared to the area, the capacitance can be found by the equation $C = \frac{\varepsilon A}{d}$, where ε is the permittivity of the dielectric material. Often, instead of being given the permittivity, we will be given the dielectric constant, κ, which is the ratio of the permittivities of the material and air, $\kappa = \frac{\varepsilon}{\varepsilon_{air}}$. This yields an obvious result of $\kappa_{air} = 1$.

The energy stored in a capacitor can be calculated in three different ways: $E = \frac{CV^2}{2} = \frac{Q^2}{2C} = \frac{VQ}{2}$. Another quantity associated with capacitors is the electric field energy density, η. This energy density is found by $\eta = \frac{\varepsilon E^2}{2}$.

CAPACITORS AND INDUCTORS IN AC CIRCUITS

Because of the constantly fluctuating nature of alternating current, capacitors and inductors both oppose immediate acceptance of the fluctuation. This opposition is referred to as **impedance** and is similar to resistance, also having units of ohms, but unlike resistance, impedance is a complex value, meaning that it may have an **imaginary component** as well as a **real component**. For ideal capacitors and inductors, impedance is purely imaginary, and for ideal resistors, impedance is purely real. It is only when combining the effects of these devices that the full expression for impedance, Z, is necessary: $Z = R + X_i$, where $i = \sqrt{(-1)}$. X is a quantity known as reactance. For capacitors, $X_c = \frac{1}{\omega C}$, where ω is the angular frequency of the current, and for inductors, $X_L = \omega L$.

RC CIRCUITS

An RC circuit consists of a battery wired in series with a **resistor** and a **capacitor**. Since a capacitor in steady state allows no current flow, it makes no sense to analyze a steady-state RC circuit. Instead, we will look at an RC circuit that has only just been connected, with the capacitor uncharged. The battery supplies voltage V_B to the circuit, and since the capacitor's voltage is initially zero, the voltage across the resistor is initially V_B, giving an initial current of $I = \frac{V_B}{R}$. As current flows, the charge on the capacitor increases, which in turn creates an opposing voltage that **lowers the voltage drop** across the resistor. Combining Ohm's Law with the KVL gives the voltage relation as $V_B = IR + \frac{Q}{C}$, where Q is the charge on the capacitor. Since the current is simply the transfer rate of the charge, this becomes a differential equation. Solving for charge and current yields the expressions $Q(t) = CV_B\left(1 - e^{-t/RC}\right)$ and $I(t) = \left(\frac{V_B}{R}\right)e^{-t/RC}$. The factor RC in the exponent is referred to as the circuit's time constant. It is the amount of time required for the capacitor to charge up to 63.2% capacity.

If the battery is removed from the circuit after the capacitor is charged and the circuit is reconnected with just the resistor and capacitor, the capacitor will begin to drain at the same rate that it was charged. The current magnitude will follow the same equation as before, though it will be in the opposite direction. The new expression for the charge will be $Q(t) = CV_B e^{-t/RC}$.

CIRCUIT ANALYSIS

When resistors in a simple circuit are arranged in **series with a battery**, current must pass through each resistor consecutively in order to return to the battery. This immediately tells us that the current through each resistor is the same. By KVL, we know that the sum of the voltage drop across the resistors is equal to the voltage input by the battery, $V_B = IR_1 + IR_2 + \cdots + IR_n$. This may be restated as $V_B = I(R_1 + R_2 + \cdots + R_n)$. From this we can see that for resistors arranged in series, the equivalent resistance is the sum of the resistances, $R_{eq} = R_1 + R_2 + \cdots + Rn$.

When resistors in a simple circuit are arranged in parallel with a battery, the current need only pass through one of them to return to the battery. By KVL, we know that the voltage drop across each resistor is the same. Since the total current must equal the sum of the currents through the resistors, we may conclude from Ohm's Law that $I = \frac{V_B}{R_1} + \frac{V_B}{R_2} + \cdots + \frac{V_B}{R_n}$. We may restate this relation as $I = V_B\left(\frac{1}{R_1} + \frac{1}{R_2} + \cdots + \frac{1}{R_n}\right)$. Moving the resistance expression to the other side of the equation shows us that the equivalent resistance is $R_{eq} = \left(\frac{1}{R_1} + \frac{1}{R_2} + \cdots + \frac{1}{R_n}\right)^{-1}$ for resistors in parallel.

Capacitors have combination rules opposite to those of resistors. **Capacitors in series** have an equivalent value of $C_{eq} = \left(\frac{1}{C_1} + \frac{1}{C_2} + \cdots + \frac{1}{C_n}\right)^{-1}$, while capacitors in parallel have equivalence of $C_{eq} = C_1 + C_2 + \cdots + C_n$.

Inductors follow the same rules as resistors.

MEASURING DEVICES

There are several devices that allow these circuit quantities to be measured to a great degree of accuracy. An **ammeter** is a device placed in series with a circuit to measure the current through that location. Ideally, an ammeter has as little internal resistance as possible to prevent altering the current it is trying to measure. A **voltmeter** measures the voltage or potential difference between two locations in a circuit. It has two leads that are connected in parallel with the circuit and consists of a very high resistance and an ammeter in series. This allows only a very small amount of current to be diverted through the voltmeter, but enough to determine the voltage by Ohm's Law. A **galvanometer** is the primary working component of an ammeter. It operates based on the idea that a wire in a magnetic field will experience a force proportional to the amount of current it is carrying. It converts the observed current into a dial reading. A **potentiometer** is a variable resistor, often controlled by a knob, that allows an operator to control the amount of voltage or current provided to a given circuit. They are commonly used in volume-control knobs. Potentiometers can also be called voltage dividers. Their use in circuit measurement is for finding voltages by comparing them to known voltages. A **multimeter** is a device that combines the functions of all the above devices into one. In addition to voltage, current, resistance and capacitance, they can typically measure inductance, frequency, and other quantities.

POWER IN AC CIRCUITS

Unlike DC circuits, the power provided by an AC voltage source is not constant over time. Generally, an AC source will provide voltage in a sinusoidal pattern, $V(t) = V_{max} \sin(\omega t)$. Similarly, the current will be given by $I(t) = I_{max} \sin(\omega t)$. From our known equations for power, this yields a power of $P(t) = R I_{max}^2 \sin^2(\omega t)$. However, if we wish to find the average power or the amount of energy transmission after a given period of time, we need to find some way to average voltage and current. The root-mean-square (rms) method, as the name suggests, takes the square root of the time average of the squared value. For sinusoidal functions such as the voltage and current here, the rms value is the maximum value divided by the square root of 2. For voltage and current, $V_{rms} = \frac{V_{max}}{\sqrt{2}}$, and $I_{rms} = \frac{I_{max}}{\sqrt{2}}$. In this way, the average power can be found as $P_{avg} = V_{rms} I_{rms}$, which can also be stated $P_{avg} = \frac{V_{max} I_{max}}{2}$. A DC source with supplied voltage V_B will provide the same power over time as an AC source if $V_B = V_{rms}$.

THE USE OF OHM'S LAW AND KIRCHHOFF'S LAWS

Circuit analysis is the process of determining the **current** or **voltage drop** across devices of interest in a circuit. Ohm's Law is useful in doing this since it definitively relates the current to the voltage drop for resistors, $V = IR$. Kirchhoff's voltage law (KVL) states that if you sum the voltage drops across all devices in any closed loop of a circuit, the sum will always be zero, $V_1 + V_2 + \cdots + V_n = 0$. This law is particularly useful if there are multiple closed-loop pathways in a circuit. Kirchhoff's current law (KCL) states that the amount of current entering a point must equal the amount of current leaving, $I_{in} = I_{out}$. This law may also be expanded to apply to the current entering and leaving a larger region of a circuit. In any given circuit analysis, it may be necessary to use all three of these laws.

Another important principle to remember in an ideal circuit is that any two points connected by only wire are at equal voltage. Only devices on the circuit may change the voltage. In actual practice, however, all wire has some amount of resistance. A battery that provides an EMF of V_B is only able to deliver a voltage to the circuit of $V = V_B - IR_B$, where R_B is the internal resistance of the battery. To express this concept in an ideal circuit, we would need to add a small resistor in series after the battery.

MAGNETS AND MAGNETISM

A **magnet** is a piece of metal, such as iron, steel, or magnetite (lodestone) that can affect another substance within its field of force that has like characteristics. Magnets can either attract or repel other substances. Magnets have two **poles**: north and south. Like poles repel and opposite poles (pairs of north and south) attract. The magnetic field is a set of invisible lines representing the paths of attraction and repulsion.

Magnetism can occur naturally, or ferromagnetic materials can be magnetized. Certain matter that is magnetized can retain its magnetic properties indefinitely and become a permanent magnet. Other matter can lose its magnetic properties. For example, an iron nail can be temporarily magnetized by stroking it repeatedly in the same direction using one pole of another magnet. Once magnetized, it can attract or repel other magnetically inclined materials, such as paper clips. Dropping the nail repeatedly will cause it to lose its magnetic properties.

Review Video: Magnets
Visit mometrix.com/academy and enter code: 570803

MAGNETIC FIELDS AND ATOMIC STRUCTURE

The motions of subatomic structures (nuclei and electrons) produce a **magnetic field**. It is the direction of the spin and orbit that indicate the direction of the field. The strength of a magnetic field is known as the magnetic moment. As electrons spin and orbit a nucleus, they produce a magnetic field.

Pairs of electrons that spin and orbit in opposite directions cancel each other out, creating a **net magnetic field** of zero. Materials that have an unpaired electron are magnetic. Those with a weak attractive force are referred to as **paramagnetic materials**, while **ferromagnetic materials** have a strong attractive force. A **diamagnetic material** has electrons that are paired, and therefore does not typically have a magnetic moment. There are, however, some diamagnetic materials that have a weak magnetic field.

A magnetic field can be formed not only by a magnetic material, but also by electric current flowing through a wire. When a coiled wire is attached to the two ends of a battery, for example, an **electromagnet** can be formed by inserting a ferromagnetic material such as an iron bar within the coil. When electric current flows through the wire, the bar becomes a magnet. If there is no current, the magnetism is lost. A **magnetic domain** occurs when the magnetic fields of atoms are grouped and aligned. These groups form what can be thought of as miniature magnets within a material. This is what happens when an object like an iron nail is temporarily magnetized. Prior to magnetization, the organization of atoms and their various polarities are somewhat random with respect to where the north and south poles are pointing. After magnetization, a significant percentage of the poles are lined up in one direction, which is what causes the magnetic force exerted by the material.

TRANSVERSE AND LONGITUDINAL WAVES

Transverse waves are waves whose oscillations are **perpendicular** to the direction of motion. A light wave is an example of a transverse wave. A group of light waves traveling in the same direction will be oscillating in several different planes. Light waves are said to be polarized when they are filtered such that only waves oscillating in a particular plane are allowed to pass, with the remainder being absorbed by the filter. If two such polarizing filters are employed successively and aligned to allow different planes of oscillation, they will block all light waves.

Longitudinal waves are waves that oscillate in the **same direction** as their primary motion. Their motion is restricted to a single axis, so they may not be polarized. A sound wave is an example of a longitudinal wave.

VELOCITY, AMPLITUDE, WAVELENGTH, AND FREQUENCY

The **velocity of a wave** is the rate at which it travels in a given medium. It is defined in the same way that velocity of physical objects is defined, a change in position divided by a change in time. A single wave may have a different velocity for every medium in which it travels. Some types of waves, such as light waves, do not require a medium.

Amplitude is one measure of a wave's strength. It is half the verticle distance between the highest and lowest points on the wave, the crest and trough, respectively. The vertical midpoint, halfway between the crest and trough, is sometimes called an equilibrium point, or a node. Amplitude is often denoted with an A.

The **wavelength** is the horizontal distance between successive crests or troughs, or the distance between the first and third of three successive nodes. Wavelength is generally denoted as λ.

Frequency is the number of crests or troughs that pass a particular point in a given period of time. It is the inverse of the period, the time required for the wave to cycle from one crest or trough to the next. Frequency, f, is generally measured in hertz, or cycles per second.

Velocity, wavelength, and frequency are not independent quantities. They are related by the expression $v = \lambda f$.

INTENSITY

Intensity is a physical quantity, equivalent to the flux through a given area over a period of time. It may also be defined as the energy density of a wave times its velocity. Intensity has units of watts per square meter. The intensity of light decreases as the distance from the light source increases. The inverse square law states that the intensity is inversely proportional to the square of the distance from the source. It is also directly proportional to the power of the light source. This is shown mathematically by the expression $I = \frac{CP}{r^2}$, where C is the proportionality constant. This may be better understood by imagining the light waves emanating from a source as an expanding sphere. As their distance from the source increases as r, the area over which they must divide themselves increases as $4\pi r^2$.

STANDING WAVES

A **standing wave** is the result of **interference** between two waves of the same frequency moving in opposite directions. These waves, although in constant motion, have certain points on the wave where the amplitude is zero, locations referred to as nodes. One example of a standing wave is a plucked guitar string. Since the string is attached at both ends, the fixed ends will be nodes. The primary tone will be that of the fundamental, or first harmonic, shown in the first figure below. It has a wavelength of twice the length of the string, L. The other three pictures below are those of the second through fourth harmonics. The nth harmonic has wavelength and frequency of $\lambda_n = \frac{2L}{n}$ and $f_n = \frac{nv}{2L}$, where v is wave velocity.

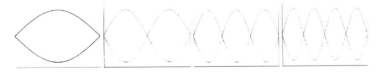

This same phenomenon occurs inside the tubes of wind instruments, though it is much more difficult to visualize. With a tube, however, there will be one or two open ends. Rather than a node, each open end will coincide with an antinode: that is, a crest or trough. For waves in a tube with two open ends, the wavelength and frequency calculations are the same as those for the plucked string. For the case with one open end, only the odd harmonics will be seen. The frequency of the nth harmonic becomes $f_n = \frac{nv}{4L}$, where n is odd.

REFLECTION, TRANSMISSION, AND ABSORPTION

When light waves make contact with matter, they are either reflected, transmitted, or absorbed. If the light is **reflected** from the surface of the matter, the **angle** at which it hits the surface will be the same as the angle at which it leaves. If the ray of light is perpendicular to the surface, it will be reflected back in the direction from which it came.

When light is **transmitted** from one medium to another, its direction may be **altered** upon entering the new medium. This is known as **refraction**. The degree to which the light is refracted depends on the speed at which light travels in each medium.

Light that is neither reflected nor transmitted will be **absorbed** by the surface and **stored as heat** energy. Because there are no ideal surfaces, most light and matter interaction will be a combination of two or even all three of these. Another result of imperfect surfaces is **scattering**, which occurs when waves are reflected in multiple directions. Rayleigh scattering is the specific case of a light wave being scattered by tiny particles that single out particular wavelengths. Dust particles in the atmosphere scatter primarily the blue wavelength of sunlight to give our sky a predominantly blue hue.

> **Review Video: Reflection, Transmission, and Absorption of Light**
> Visit mometrix.com/academy and enter code: 109410

SNELL'S LAW

When light is transmitted from one medium to another, its direction may be altered upon entering the new medium. This is known as **refraction**. The degree to which the light is refracted depends on the index of refraction, n, for each medium. The **index of refraction** is a ratio of the speed of light in a vacuum to the speed of light in the medium in question, $n = \frac{c}{v_m}$. Since light can never travel faster than it does in a vacuum, the index of refraction is always greater than one. Snell's law gives the equation for determining the angle of refraction: $n_1 \sin(\theta_1) = n_2 \sin(\theta_2)$, where n is the index of refraction for each medium, and θ is the angle the light makes with the normal vector on each side of the interface between the two media.

We will examine a special case by trying to determine the angle of refraction for light traveling from a medium with $n_1 = 3$ to another medium with $n_2 = 1.5$. The light makes an angle $\theta_1 = 35°$ with the normal. Using Snell's law, we find that $\sin(\theta_2) = 1.15$. Since this is not mathematically possible, we conclude that the light cannot be refracted. This case is known as total internal reflection. When light travels from a more dense medium to a less dense medium, there is a minimum angle of incidence, beyond which all light will be reflected. This critical angle is $\theta_1 = \sin^{-1}\left(\frac{n_2}{n_1}\right)$. Fiber-optic cables make use of this phenomenon to ensure that the signal is fully reflected internally when it veers into the outer walls of the fiber.

RESONANCE AND NATURAL FREQUENCY

Every physical object has one or more **natural frequencies**, or frequencies at which it will naturally vibrate. The natural frequency is based on the object's dimensions, density, orientation, and other factors. If the object is acted on by a periodic force, it will vibrate at its natural frequency, regardless of the forcing frequency. If the excitation force is operating at the object's natural frequency, the object will experience **resonance**, in which the object receives all of the energy exerted by the excitation force. The amplitude of the vibration will increase rapidly and without bound until either the excitation force changes frequency or the natural frequency of the object is altered.

DIFFRACTION AND DISPERSION

Diffraction occurs when a wave encounters a physical object. It includes phenomena such as bending, diverging, and other aperture effects. When light emerges from a single small slit, a rippling effect may be observed. The results of Young's double-slit experiment are due to diffraction as the light waves from these slits diverge. Similarly, light emerging from a circular aperture will project concentric light and dark rings due to diffraction. Diffraction grating is an arrangement of material whose reflective properties are intentionally varied at equally spaced intervals. Due to the arrangement, incident light is reflected in specific directions, known as diffraction orders, based on its wavelength.

Dispersion occurs when light consisting of multiple wavelengths enters a medium whose propagation behavior depends on the wavelength of transmitted light. This is what is observed when light passes through a prism, splitting it into its component colors.

> **Review Video: Diffraction of Light Waves**
> Visit mometrix.com/academy and enter code: 785494

YOUNG'S DOUBLE-SLIT EXPERIMENT

Thomas Young's **double-slit experiment** visually demonstrated the interference between two sets of light waves. It consisted of shining light through two thin, closely spaced parallel slits and onto a screen. The interference between light waves from the two slits caused a pattern of alternately light and dark bands to appear on the screen, due to constructive and destructive interference, respectively. The dimensions of the experimental setup can be used to determine the wavelength of the light being projected onto the screen. This is given by the equation $\lambda = y\frac{d}{x}$, where y is the distance between the centers of two light bands, d is the distance between the slits, and x is the distance from the slits to the screen. Thin-film interference is caused when incident light is reflected both by a partially reflective thin layer on a surface and by the surface itself. This interference may be constructive or destructive.

WAVE SUPERPOSITION AND INTERFERENCE

The principle of **linear superposition** states that two or more waves occupying the same space create an effect equal to the sum of their individual amplitudes at that location. This is known as interference. If the resultant amplitude is larger than either individual amplitude, it is constructive interference. Similarly, if the interference reduces the effect, it is considered destructive.

Some special cases of interference are standing waves and beats, in which two waves having the same and nearly the same frequency, respectively, interfere with one another. Another concept related to interference is phase. If two waves with the same frequency are in phase, then they have perfectly constructive interference. The nodes in each wave will line up, as will the respective crests and troughs. If those same two waves are 180 degrees out of phase, they will experience perfectly destructive interference. The nodes will still line up, but each crest will be aligned with a trough, and vice versa. From this it can be seen that constructive interference results in a larger wave amplitude than destructive interference. If two identical waves are 180 degrees out of phase, the resultant wave will have zero amplitude. This effect is the design impetus for some noise-cancellation technology.

DOPPLER EFFECT

One common phenomenon of wave motion is the **Doppler effect**. It is a **disparity** between the emitted frequency and the observed frequency. It is the caused by **relative motion** between the

wave source and the **observer**. If the source and observer are both moving toward one another, the observed frequency is determined by the following equation: $f_o = f_e \frac{(v_w + v_o)}{(v_w - v_s)}$, where v_w is the speed of the wave. If the source or the observer is moving in the opposite direction, its sign must be reversed. The Doppler effect is most commonly observed when sound waves change pitch as an observer's relative motion to a train or emergency vehicle changes. The Doppler effect is also employed in the operation of speed-detecting radar guns. Microwaves are emitted at a known frequency and, after being reflected by the object in question, return at a different frequency, giving the object's speed.

SOUND WAVES

The **pitch of a sound** as it reaches one's ear is based on the frequency of the sound waves. A high-pitched sound has a higher frequency than a low-pitched sound. Like all waves, sound waves transmit energy. The rate at which this energy is transmitted is the sonic power. Loudness, or intensity of sound, is the sonic power received per unit area.

Beats occur when a pair of sound waves, whose frequencies differ only slightly, interfere with one another. This interference causes a periodic variation in sound intensity, whose frequency is equal to the difference between that of the two sound waves. This is noticeable when tuning two instruments to one another. As the two pitches get closer, the beat frequency will become smaller and smaller until it disappears entirely, indicating that the instruments are in tune.

> **Review Video: Sound**
> Visit mometrix.com/academy and enter code: 562378

ELECTROMAGNETIC SPECTRUM

The **electromagnetic spectrum** is the range of all wavelengths and frequencies of known electromagnetic waves. Visible light occupies only a small portion of the electromagnetic spectrum. Some of the common classifications of electromagnetic waves are listed in the table below with their approximate frequency ranges.

Classification	Freq. (Hz)
Gamma Rays	$\sim 10^{19}$
X-Rays	$\sim 10^{17} - 10^{18}$
Ultraviolet	$\sim 10^{15} - 10^{16}$
Visible Light	$\sim 10^{14}$
Infra-red	$\sim 10^{11} - 10^{14}$
Microwaves	$\sim 10^{10} - 10^{11}$
Radio/TV	$\sim 10^{6} - 10^{9}$

Electromagnetic waves travel at the speed of light, $c = 3 \times 10^8$ m/s. To find the wavelength of any electromagnetic wave, simply divide c by the frequency. Visible light occupies a range of wavelengths from approximately 380 nm (violet) to 740 nm (red). The full spectrum of color can be found between these two wavelengths.

> **Review Video: Electromagnetic Spectrum**
> Visit mometrix.com/academy and enter code: 771761
>
> **Review Video: Light**
> Visit mometrix.com/academy and enter code: 900556

REAL AND VIRTUAL IMAGES

In optics, an **object's image** is what is seen when the object is viewed through a lens. The location of an object's image is related to the lens's **focal length** by the equation $\frac{1}{d_o} + \frac{1}{d_i} = \frac{1}{f}$, where f is the focal length, and d_o and d_i are the distance of the object and its image from the lens, respectively. A positive d_i indicates that the image is on the opposite side of the lens from the object. If the lens is a magnifying lens, the height of the object may be different from that of its image, and may even be inverted. The object's magnification, m, can be found as $m = \frac{-d_i}{d_o}$. The value for the magnification can then be used to relate the object's height to that of its image: $m = \frac{y_i}{y_o}$. Note that if the magnification is negative, then the image has been inverted.

Images may be either **real** or **virtual**. Real images are formed by light rays passing through the image location, while virtual images are only perceived by reverse extrapolating refracted light rays. Diverging lenses cannot create real images, only virtual ones. Real images are always on the opposite side of a converging lens from the object and are always inverted.

THIN LENSES

A **lens** is an optical device that **redirects light** to either converge or diverge in specific geometric patterns. Whether the lens converges or diverges is dependent on the lens being **convex** or **concave**, respectively. The particular angle of redirection is dictated by the lens's focal length. For a **converging lens**, this is the distance from the lens that parallel rays entering from the opposite side would intersect. For a **diverging lens**, it is the distance from the lens that parallel rays entering the lens would intersect if they were reverse extrapolated. However, the focal length of a diverging lens is always considered to be negative. A thin lens is a lens whose focal length is much greater than its thickness. By making this assumption, we can derive many helpful relations.

CONCAVE MIRRORS

Concave mirrors will create an image of an object in varying ways depending on the location of the object. The table below details the location, orientation, magnification, and nature of the image. The five object locations to be examined are between the mirror and the focal point (1), at the focal point (2), between the focal point and the center of curvature, or twice the focal point (3), at the center of curvature (4), and beyond the center of curvature (5).

Object	Image Location	Orientation	Magnification	Type
1	$d_i < 0$	upright	$m > 1$	virtual
2	none	none	none	none
3	$d_i > 2f$	inverted	$m < -1$	real
4	$d_i = 2f$	inverted	$m = -1$	real
5	$f < d_i < 2f$	inverted	$0 > m > -1$	real

Note in case 5 that the image may effectively be located at the focal point. This is the case for objects at extremely great, or near infinite, distances from the mirror. The magnification at these distances will be very small and a true infinite distance would result in a magnification of zero.

PLANE MIRRORS AND SPHERICAL MIRRORS

Plane mirrors have very simple properties. They reflect only **virtual images**, they have no magnification, and the object's distance from the mirror is always equal to that of its image. Plane mirrors will also appear to reverse the directions left and right.

Spherical mirrors follow the same governing equations for finding image height, location, orientation, and magnification as do thin lenses; however, the sign convention for image location is reversed. A positive image location denotes that it is on the same side as the object. Spherical mirrors may be either **concave** or **convex**. Convex mirrors are by far the simpler of the two. They will always reflect virtual, upright images with magnification between zero and one. Concave mirrors have varying behavior based on the object location.

SIMPLE MAGNIFIER, THE MICROSCOPE, AND THE TELESCOPE

A simple magnifier, or commonly a **magnifying glass**, is a converging lens that creates an enlarged virtual image near the observer's eye. The object must be within a certain distance, about 25 cm or 10 inches, from the magnifier for it to operate properly. Otherwise, the image will be blurry.

A **microscope** is a magnifying device that is used to examine very small objects. It uses a series of lenses to capture light coming from the far side of the sample under examination. Often microscopes will have interchangeable magnification lenses mounted on a wheel, allowing the user to adjust the level of magnification by rotating in a different lens. Optical microscopes will generally be limited to a magnification of 1,500.

Telescopes are used to view very distant objects, most often celestial bodies. Telescopes use both lenses and mirrors to capture light from a distant source, focus it, and then magnify it. This creates a virtual image that is very much smaller than the object itself, and yet much larger than the object appears to the naked eye.

PRISMS

Prisms are optical devices that alter the path or nature of light waves. Glass and plastic are the two most prevalent materials used to make prisms. There are three different types of prisms in common use. The most familiar of these is the dispersive prism, which splits a beam of light into its constituent wavelengths. For sunlight, this results in the full spectrum of color being displayed. These prisms are generally in the familiar triangular prism shape.

Polarizing prisms, as their name suggests, polarize light, but without significantly reducing the intensity, as a simple filter would. Waves that are oscillating in planes other than the desired plane are caused to rotate, so that they are oscillating in the desired plane. This type of prism is commonly used in cameras.

Reflective prisms are much less common than either of the others. They reflect light, often through the use of the total internal reflection phenomenon. Their primary use is in binoculars.

HEAT TRANSFER

Heat transfer is the flow of thermal energy, which is measured by temperature. Heat will flow from warmer objects to cooler objects until an **equilibrium** is reached in which both objects are at the same temperature. Because the particles of warmer objects possess a higher kinetic energy than the particles of cooler objects, the particles of the warmer objects are vibrating more quickly and collide more often, transferring energy to the cooler objects in which the particles have less kinetic energy and are moving more slowly. Heat may be transferred by conduction, convection, or radiation. In **conduction**, heat is transferred by direct contact between two objects. In **convection**, heat is transferred by moving currents. In **radiation**, heat is transferred by electromagnetic waves.

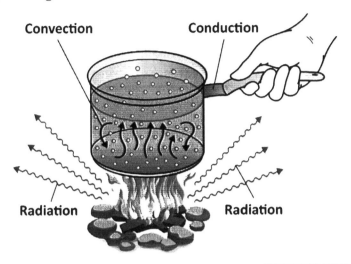

CONVECTION

Heat always flows from a region of higher temperature to a region of lower temperature. If two regions are at the same temperature, there is a thermal equilibrium between them and there will be no net heat transfer between them. Convection is a mode of heat transfer in which a surface in contact with a fluid experiences a heat flow. The heat rate for convection is given as $q = hA\Delta T$, where h is the convection coefficient, and q is the heat transferred per unit of time. The convection coefficient is dependent on a number of factors, including the configuration of the surface and the nature and velocity of the fluid. For complicated configurations, it often has to be determined experimentally.

Convection may be classified as either free or forced. In free convection, when a surface transfers heat to the surrounding air, the heated air becomes less dense and rises, allowing cooler air to descend and come into contact with the surface. Free convection may also be called natural convection. Forced convection in this example would involve forcibly cycling the air: for instance, with a fan. While this does generally require an additional input of work, the convection coefficient is always greater for forced convection.

CONDUCTION

Conduction is a form of heat transfer that requires contact. Since heat is a measure of kinetic energy, most commonly vibration, at the atomic level, it may be transferred from one location to another or one object to another by contact. The rate at which heat is transferred is proportional to the material's thermal conductivity k, cross-sectional area A, and temperature gradient $\frac{\Delta T}{\Delta x}$:

$$q = kA\left(\frac{\Delta T}{\Delta x}\right)$$

If two ends of a rod are each held at a constant temperature, the heat transfer through the rod will be given as $q = kA\left(\frac{T_H - T_L}{d}\right)$, where d is the length of the rod. The heat will flow from the hot end to the cold end. The thermal conductivity is generally given in units of $\frac{W}{m\,K}$. Metals are some of the best conductors, many having a thermal conductivity around $400\ \frac{W}{m\,K}$. The thermal conductivity of wood is very small, generally less than $0.5\ \frac{W}{m\,K}$. Diamond is extremely thermally conductive and may have a conductivity of over $2,000\ \frac{W}{m\,K}$. Although fluids also have thermal conductivity, they will tend to transfer heat primarily through convection.

RADIATION

Radiation heat transfer occurs via electromagnetic radiation between two bodies. Unlike conduction and convection, radiation requires no medium in which to take place. Indeed, the heat we receive from the sun is entirely radiation since it must pass through a vacuum to reach us. Every body at a temperature above absolute zero emits heat radiation at a rate of $q = e\sigma A T^4$, where e is the surface emissivity and σ is the Stefan-Boltzmann constant. The net radiation heat-transfer rate for a body is given by $q = e\sigma A(T^4 - T_0^4)$, where T_0 is the temperature of the surroundings. Emissivity, which has a value between 0 and 1, is a measure of how well a surface absorbs and emits radiation. Dark-colored surfaces tend to have high emissivity, while shiny or reflective surfaces have low emissivity. In the radiation heat-rate equation, it is important to remember to use absolute temperature units, since the temperature value is being raised to a power.

CHEMICAL, ELECTRICAL, ELECTROMAGNETIC, NUCLEAR, AND THERMAL ENERGY

Different types of energy may be associated with systems:

- **Chemical energy** is the energy that is stored in chemical bonds and intermolecular forces.
- **Electrical energy** is the energy associated with the movement of electrons or ions through a material.
- **Electromagnetic energy** is the energy of electromagnetic waves of several frequencies including radio waves, microwaves, infrared light, visible light, ultraviolet light, x-rays, and gamma rays.
- **Nuclear energy** is the binding energy that is stored within an atom's nucleus.
- **Thermal energy** is the total internal kinetic energy of a system due to the random motions of the particles.

STATES OF MATTER

The four states of matter are solid, liquid, gas, and plasma. **Solids** have a definite shape and a definite volume. Because solid particles are held in fairly rigid positions, solids are the least compressible of the four states of matter. **Liquids** have definite volumes but no definite shapes. Because their particles are free to slip and slide over each other, liquids take the shape of their containers, but they still remain fairly incompressible by natural means. **Gases** have no definite shape or volume. Because gas particles are free to move, they move away from each other to fill their containers. Gases are compressible. **Plasmas** are high-temperature, ionized gases that exist only under very high temperatures at which electrons are stripped away from their atoms.

> **Review Video: States of Matter**
> Visit mometrix.com/academy and enter code: 742449
>
> **Review Video: Properties of Liquids**
> Visit mometrix.com/academy and enter code: 802024

The following table shows similarities and differences between solids, liquids, and gases:

	Solid	Liquid	Gas
Shape	Fixed shape	No fixed shape (assumes shape of container)	No fixed shape (assumes shape of container)
Volume	Fixed	Fixed	Changes to assume shape of container
Fluidity	Does not flow easily	Flows easily	Flows easily
Compressibility	Hard to compress	Hard to compress	Compresses

SIX DIFFERENT TYPES OF PHASE CHANGE

A substance that is undergoing a change from a solid to a liquid is said to be melting. If this change occurs in the opposite direction, from liquid to solid, this change is called freezing. A liquid which is being converted to a gas is undergoing vaporization. The reverse of this process is known as condensation. Direct transitions from gas to solid and solid to gas are much less common in everyday life, but they can occur given the proper conditions. Solid to gas conversion is known as sublimation, while the reverse is called deposition.

PHASE DIAGRAM AND CRITICAL POINT

A **phase diagram** is a graph or chart of pressure versus temperature that represents the solid, liquid, and gaseous phases of a substance and the transitions between these phases. Typically, **pressure** is located on the vertical axis, and temperature is located along the horizontal axis. The curves drawn on the graph represent points at which different phases are in an equilibrium state. These curves indicate at which pressure and temperature the phase changes of sublimation, melting, and boiling occur. Specifically, the curve between the liquid and gas phases indicates the pressures and temperatures at which the liquid and gas phases are in equilibrium. The curve between the solid and liquid phases indicates the temperatures and pressures at which the solid and liquid phases are in equilibrium. The open spaces on the graph represent the distinct phases solid, liquid, and gas. The point on the curve at which the graph splits is referred to as the **critical point**. At the critical point, the solid, liquid, and gas phases all exist in a state of equilibrium.

LETTERED REGIONS OF A PHASE DIAGRAM

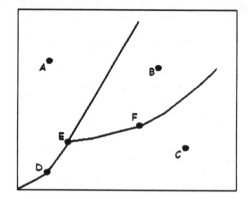

A—**Solid phase**: This is a region of high pressure and low temperature where the substance always exists as a solid.

B—**Liquid phase**: This is a region of pressure and temperature where the substance is in the liquid phase.

C—**Gas phase**: This is a region of pressure and temperature where the substance is in the gaseous phase.

D—**Sublimation point**: The portion of the curve that contains point D shows all the combinations of pressure and temperature at which the solid phase is in equilibrium with the gaseous phase.

E—**Critical point**: The point at which the solid, liquid, and gaseous phases are all in equilibrium.

F—**Boiling point**: The line that contains point F indicates all the combinations of pressure and temperature at which the liquid phase and gas phase are in equilibrium.

LAWS OF THERMODYNAMICS

FIRST LAW

The **first law of thermodynamics** states that energy cannot be **created** or **destroyed**, but only **converted** from one form to another. It is generally applied as $Q = \Delta U + W$, where Q is the net heat energy added to a system, ΔU is the change in internal energy of the system, and W is the work done by the system. For any input of heat energy to a system, that energy must be either converted to internal energy through a temperature increase or expended in doing work. For a system that gives off heat, either the temperature of the system must decrease or work must be done on the system by its surroundings. By convention, work done by the system is positive while work done on the system is negative.

For instance, suppose a gas is compressed by a piston while the gas temperature remains constant. If we consider the gas to be the system, the work is negative, since the work is being performed on the gas. Since the temperature remains constant, $\Delta U = 0$. Thus, Q must be a negative quantity, indicating that heat is lost by the gas. Conversely, if the gas does positive work on the piston while remaining at a constant temperature, the gas must be receiving heat input from the surroundings.

SECOND LAW

The **second law of thermodynamics** is primarily a statement of the natural tendency of all things toward disorder rather than order. It deals with a quantity called **entropy**, which is an inverse measure of the remaining useful energy in a system. If we take a system of a pot of hot water and an ice cube, the system entropy initially has a value of s_1. After the ice cube melts in the water and the system reaches an equilibrium temperature, the system has larger entropy value s_2, which is the maximum entropy for the system. The system cannot return to its initial state without work put into the system to refreeze the ice cube and reheat the water. If this is done and the system returns to a state with entropy s_1, then the entropy of the surroundings must at the same time increase by more than $s_2 - s_1$, since the net entropy from any process is always greater than zero. Reversible processes are those that may be accomplished in reverse without requiring additional work input. These processes do not exist in the real world, but can be useful for approximating some situations. All real processes are irreversible, meaning they require additional work input to accomplish in reverse. Another important concept is that of spontaneity, the ability of a process to occur without instigation. An ice cube located in an environment at a temperature above the freezing point will spontaneously melt. Although some processes can decrease system entropy at a cost to the entropy of the surroundings, all spontaneous processes involve an increase in system entropy.

THIRD AND ZEROTH LAWS

The **third law of thermodynamics** regards the behavior of systems as they **approach absolute zero temperature**. Actually reaching a state of absolute zero is impossible. According to this law, all activity disappears as molecules slow to a standstill near absolute zero, and the system achieves a perfect crystal structure while the system entropy approaches its minimum value. For most systems, this would in fact be a value of zero entropy. Note that this does not violate the second law since causing a system to approach absolute zero would require an immense increase in the entropy of the surroundings, resulting in a positive net entropy. This law is used to determine the value of a material's standard entropy, which is its entropy at the standard temperature of 25 °C.

The **zeroth law of thermodynamics** deals with thermal equilibrium between two systems. It states that if two systems are both in thermal equilibrium with a third system, then they are in thermal equilibrium with each other. This may seem intuitive, but it is an important basis for the other thermodynamic laws.

> **Review Video: Laws of Thermodynamics**
> Visit mometrix.com/academy and enter code: 253607

ENTROPY

Entropy (S) is the amount of **disorder** or **randomness of a system**. According to the second law of thermodynamics, systems tend toward a state of greater entropy. The second law of thermodynamics can also be stated as $\Delta S > 0$. Processes with positive changes in entropy tend to be spontaneous. For example, melting is a process with a positive ΔS. When a solid changes into a liquid state, the substance becomes more disordered; therefore, entropy increases. Entropy also will increase in a reaction in which the number of moles of gases increases due to the amount of disorder increasing. Entropy increases when a solute dissolves into a solvent due to the increase in the number of particles. Entropy increases when a system is heated due to the particles moving faster and the amount of disorder increasing.

SPONTANEOUS / REVERSIBLE PROCESSES

Some chemical processes are **spontaneous**. According to the second law of thermodynamics, systems or processes always **tend to a state of greater entropy** or lower potential energy. Some exothermic chemical systems are spontaneous because they can increase their stability by reaching a lower potential energy. If processes or reactions have products at a lower potential energy, these processes tend to be spontaneous. Spontaneous reactions have only one direction as given by the second law of thermodynamics. Spontaneous processes go in the direction of greater entropy and lower potential energy. To be reversible, a reaction or process has to be able to go back and forth between two states. A spontaneous process is irreversible.

CONCEPT OF CHANGE IN ENTHALPY

All chemical processes involve either the release or the absorption of heat. Enthalpy is this heat energy. **Enthalpy** is a state function that is equivalent to the amount of heat a system exchanges with its surroundings. For **exothermic processes**, which release heat, the change in enthalpy (ΔH) is negative because the final enthalpy is less than the initial enthalpy. For **endothermic processes**, which absorb heat, the change in enthalpy (ΔH) is positive because the final enthalpy is greater than the initial enthalpy.

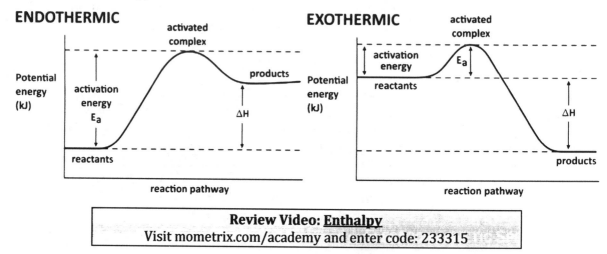

Review Video: Enthalpy
Visit mometrix.com/academy and enter code: 233315

GIBBS ENERGY

Gibbs energy (G), also known as Gibbs free energy, is the energy of the system that is available to do work. Gibbs energy determines the **spontaneity** of chemical and physical processes. Some processes are spontaneous because $\Delta H < 0$ or because $\Delta S > 0$. If one of the conditions is favorable but the other condition is not favorable, Gibbs energy can be used to determine if a process is spontaneous. Gibbs energy is given by $G = H - TS$. For processes that occur at constant temperature, $\Delta G = \Delta H - T\Delta S$. If ΔG is equal to zero, then the reaction is at equilibrium and neither the forward nor the reverse reaction is spontaneous. If ΔG is less than zero, then the forward reaction is spontaneous. If ΔG is greater than zero, then the reverse reaction is spontaneous.

Chemistry

ATOMIC MODELS AND THEORIES

There have been many theories regarding the **structure** of atoms and their particles. Part of the challenge in developing an understanding of matter is that atoms and their particles are too small to be seen. It is believed that the first conceptualization of the atom was developed by **Democritus** in 400 B.C. Some of the more notable models are the solid sphere or billiard ball model postulated by **John Dalton**, the plum pudding or raisin bun model by **J.J. Thomson**, the planetary or nuclear model by **Ernest Rutherford**, the Bohr or orbit model by **Niels Bohr**, and the electron cloud or quantum mechanical model by **Louis de Broglie** and **Erwin Schrodinger**. Rutherford directed the alpha scattering experiment that discounted the plum pudding model. The shortcoming of the Bohr model was the belief that electrons orbited in fixed rather than changing ecliptic orbits.

Review Video: Atomic Models
Visit mometrix.com/academy and enter code: 434851

Review Video: John Dalton
Visit mometrix.com/academy and enter code: 565627

THOMSON "PLUM PUDDING" MODEL

J.J. Thomson, the discoverer of the electron, suggested that the arrangement of protons and electrons within an atom could be approximated by dried fruit in a **plum pudding**. Thomson, whose discovery of the electron preceded that of the proton or neutron, hypothesized that an atom's electrons, the dried plums, were positioned uniformly inside the atom within a cloud of positive charge, the pudding. This model was later disproved.

RUTHERFORD SCATTERING

Ernest Rutherford concluded from the work of Geiger and Marsden that the majority of the mass was concentrated in a minute, positively charged region, the **nucleus**, which was surrounded by **electrons**. When a positive alpha particle approached close enough to the nucleus, it was strongly repelled, enough so that it had the ability to rebound at high angles. The small nucleus size explained the small number of alpha particles that were repelled in this fashion. The scattering led to development of the **planetary model of the atom**, which was further developed by Niels Bohr into what is now known as the Bohr model.

BOHR MODEL

Niels Bohr postulated that the electrons orbiting the nucleus must occupy discrete orbits. These discrete orbits also corresponded to discrete levels of energy and angular momentum. Consequently, the only way that electrons could move between orbits was by making nearly instantaneous jumps between them. These jumps, known as **quantum leaps**, are associated with the absorption or emission of a quantum of energy, known as a photon. If the electron is jumping to a higher energy state, a photon must be absorbed. Similarly, if the electron is dropping to a lower energy state, a photon must be emitted.

Review Video: Structure of Atoms
Visit mometrix.com/academy and enter code: 905932

BASIC ORGANIZATION OF MATTER

An **element** is the most basic type of matter. It has unique properties and cannot be broken down into other elements. The smallest unit of an element is the **atom**. A chemical combination of two or more types of elements is called a compound. **Compounds** often have properties that are very different from those of their constituent elements. The smallest independent unit of an element or compound is known as a **molecule**. Most elements are found somewhere in nature in single-atom form, but a few elements only exist naturally in pairs. These are called diatomic elements, of which some of the most common are hydrogen, nitrogen, and oxygen. Elements and compounds are represented by chemical symbols, one or two letters, most often the first in the element name. More than one atom of the same element in a compound is represented with a subscript number designating how many atoms of that element are present. Water, for instance, contains two hydrogens and one oxygen. Thus, the chemical formula is H_2O. Methane contains one carbon and four hydrogens, so its formula is CH_4.

Review Video: Molecules
Visit mometrix.com/academy and enter code: 349910

PROTONS, NEUTRONS, AND ELECTRONS

The three major subatomic particles are the proton, neutron, and electron. The **proton**, which is located in the nucleus, has a relative charge of $+1$. The **neutron**, which is located in the nucleus, has a relative charge of 0. The **electron**, which is located outside the nucleus, has a relative charge of -1. The proton and neutron, which are essentially the same mass, are much more massive than the electron and make up the mass of the atom. The electron's mass is insignificant compared to the mass of the proton and neutron.

ORBITS AND ORBITALS

An **orbit** is a definite path, but an orbital is a region in space. The Bohr model described electrons as orbiting or following a definite path in space around the nucleus of an atom. But, according to **Heisenberg's uncertainty principle**, it is impossible to determine the location and the momentum of an electron simultaneously. Therefore, it is impossible to draw a definite path or orbit of an electron. An **orbital** as described by the quantum-mechanical model or the electron-cloud model is a region in space that is drawn in such a way as to indicate the probability of finding an electron at a specific location. The distance an orbital is located from the nucleus corresponds to the principal quantum number. The orbital shape corresponds to the subshell or azimuthal quantum number. The orbital orientation corresponds to the magnetic quantum number.

QUANTUM NUMBERS

The **principal quantum number** (n) describes an electron's shell or energy level and actually describes the size of the orbital. Electrons farther from the nucleus are at higher energy levels. The **subshell** or azimuthal quantum number (l) describes the electron's sublevel or subshell (s, p, d, or f) and specifies the shape of the orbital. Typical shapes include spherical, dumbbell, and clover leaf. The **magnetic quantum number** (m_l) describes the orientation of the orbital in space. The spin or magnetic moment quantum number (m_s) describes the direction of the spin of the electron in the orbital.

ATOMIC NUMBER AND MASS NUMBER

The **atomic number** of an element is the number of protons in the nucleus of an atom of that element. This is the number that identifies the type of an atom. For example, all oxygen atoms have eight protons, and all carbon atoms have six protons. Each element is identified by its specific atomic number.

The **mass number** is the number of protons and neutrons in the nucleus of an atom. Although the atomic number is the same for all atoms of a specific element, the mass number can vary due to the varying numbers of neutrons in various isotopes of the atom.

ISOTOPES

Isotopes are atoms of the same element that vary in their number of neutrons. Isotopes of the same element have the same number of protons and thus the same atomic number. But, because isotopes vary in the number of neutrons, they can be identified by their mass numbers. For example, two naturally occurring carbon isotopes are carbon-12 and carbon-13, which have mass numbers 12 and 13, respectively. The symbols $^{12}_{6}C$ and $^{13}_{6}C$ also represent the carbon isotopes. The general form of the symbol is $^{M}_{A}X$, where X represents the element symbol, M represents the mass number, and A represents the atomic number.

AVERAGE ATOMIC MASS

The **average atomic mass** is the weighted average of the masses of all the naturally occurring isotopes of an atom in comparison to the carbon-12 isotope. The unit for average atomic mass is the atomic mass unit (u). Atomic masses of isotopes are measured using a mass spectrometer by bombarding a gaseous sample of the isotope and measuring its relative deflections. Atomic masses can be calculated if the percent abundances and the atomic masses of the naturally occurring isotopes are known.

CATHODE RAY TUBE (CRT)

Electrons were discovered by Joseph John Thomson through scientific work with cathode ray tubes (CRTs). **Cathode rays** had been studied for many years, but it was Thomson who showed that cathode rays were **negatively charged particles**. Although Thomson could not determine an electron's charge or mass, he was able to determine the ratio of the charge to the mass. Thomson discovered that this ratio was constant regardless of the gas in the CRT. He was able to show that the cathode rays were actually streams of negatively charged particles by deflecting them with a positively charged plate.

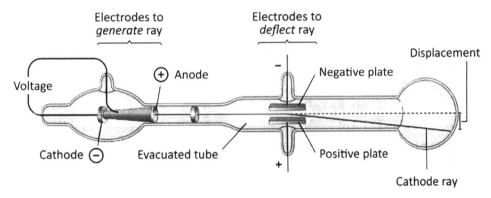

GOLD FOIL EXPERIMENT

After Thomson determined the ratio of the charge to the mass of an electron from studying cathode rays, he proposed the plum pudding model, in which he compared electrons to the raisins embedded in plum pudding. This model of the atom was disproved by the gold foil experiment. The gold foil experiment led to the discovery of the nucleus of an atom. Scientists at Rutherford's laboratory bombarded a thin gold foil with high-speed helium ions. Much to their surprise, some of the ions were reflected by the foil. The scientists concluded that the atom has a **hard central core**, which we now know to be the **nucleus**.

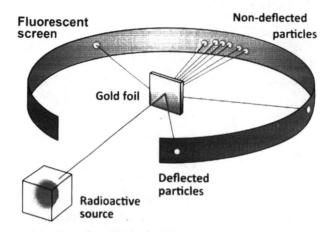

PROBLEMS THAT RUTHERFORD'S MODEL HAD WITH SPECTRAL LINES

Rutherford's model allowed for the electrons of an atom to be in an **infinite number of orbits** based on Newton's laws of motion. Rutherford believed that electrons could orbit the nucleus at any distance from the nucleus and that electrons could change velocity and direction at any moment. But, according to Rutherford's model, the electrons would lose energy and spiral into the nucleus. Unfortunately, if this was in fact true, then every atom would be **unstable**. Rutherford's model also does not correspond to the spectral lines emitted from gases at low pressure. The **spectral lines** are discrete bands of light at specific energy levels. These spectral lines indicate that electrons must be at specific distances from the nucleus. If electrons could be located at any distance from the nucleus, then these gases should emit continuous spectra instead of spectral lines.

PURE SUBSTANCES

Pure substances are substances that cannot be further broken down into simpler substances and still retain their characteristics. Pure substances are categorized as either **elements** or **compounds**. Elements that consist of only one type of atom may be monatomic, diatomic, or polyatomic. For example, helium (He) and copper (Cu) are monatomic elements, and hydrogen (H_2) and oxygen (O_2) are diatomic elements. Phosphorus (P_4) and sulfur (S_8) are polyatomic elements. Compounds consist of molecules of more than one type of atom. For example, pure water (H_2O) is made up of molecules consisting of two atoms of hydrogen bonded to one atom of oxygen, and glucose ($C_6H_{12}O_6$) is made up of molecules of six carbon atoms and twelve hydrogen atoms bonded together with six oxygen atoms.

MIXTURES

Mixtures can be classified as either homogeneous mixtures or heterogeneous mixtures. The molecules of **homogeneous mixtures** are distributed uniformly throughout the mixture, but the molecules of **heterogeneous mixtures** are not distributed uniformly throughout the mixture. Air is an example of a homogeneous mixture, and a pile of sand and rock is an example of a heterogeneous mixture. Solutions are homogeneous mixtures consisting of a **solute** (the substance that is dissolved) and a **solvent** (the substance doing the dissolving).

SUSPENSIONS

Suspensions are heterogeneous mixtures in which the particle size of the substance **suspended** is too large to be kept in suspension by Brownian motion. Once left undisturbed, suspensions will settle out to form layers. An example of a suspension is sand stirred into water. Left undisturbed, the sand will fall out of suspension and the water will form a layer on top of the sand.

MIXTURES WITH COMPOUNDS

Mixtures are similar to compounds in that they are produced when two or more substances are combined. However, there are some key differences as well. Compounds require a chemical combination of the constituent particles, while mixtures are simply the interspersion of particles. Unlike compounds, mixtures may be **separated** without a chemical change. A mixture retains the chemical properties of its constitutent particles, while a compound acquires a new set of properties. Given compounds can exist only in specific ratios, while mixtures may be any ratio of the involved substances.

CHEMICAL AND PHYSICAL PROPERTIES

Matter has both physical and chemical properties. **Physical properties** can be seen or observed without changing the identity or composition of matter. For example, the mass, volume, and density of a substance can be determined without permanently changing the sample. Other physical properties include color, boiling point, freezing point, solubility, odor, hardness, electrical conductivity, thermal conductivity, ductility, and malleability.

Chemical properties cannot be measured without changing the identity or composition of matter. Chemical properties describe how a substance reacts or changes to form a new substance. Examples of chemical properties include flammability, corrosivity, oxidation states, enthalpy of formation, and reactivity with other chemicals.

INTENSIVE AND EXTENSIVE PROPERTIES

Physical properties are categorized as either intensive or extensive. **Intensive properties** *do not* depend on the amount of matter or quantity of the sample. This means that intensive properties will not change if the sample size is increased or decreased. Intensive properties include color, hardness, melting point, boiling point, density, ductility, malleability, specific heat, temperature, concentration, and magnetization.

Extensive properties *do* depend on the amount of matter or quantity of the sample. Therefore, extensive properties do change if the sample size is increased or decreased. If the sample size is increased, the property increases. If the sample size is decreased, the property decreases. Extensive properties include volume, mass, weight, energy, entropy, number of moles, and electrical charge.

ATOMIC PROPERTIES OF NEUTRAL ATOMS, ANIONS, AND CATIONS

Neutral atoms have equal numbers of protons and electrons. **Cations** are positively-charged ions that are formed when atoms lose electrons in order to have a full outer shell of valence electrons. For example, the alkali metals sodium and potassium form the cations Na^+ and K^+, and the alkaline earth metals magnesium and calcium form the cations Mg^{2+} and Ca^{2+}.

Anions are negatively-charged ions that are formed when atoms gain electrons to fill their outer shell of valence electrons. For example, the halogens fluorine and chlorine form the anions F^- and Cl^-.

CHEMICAL AND PHYSICAL CHANGES

Physical changes do not produce new substances. The atoms or molecules may be rearranged, but no new substances are formed. **Phase changes** or changes of state such as melting, freezing, and

33

sublimation are physical changes. For example, physical changes include the melting of ice, the boiling of water, sugar dissolving into water, and the crushing of a piece of chalk into a fine powder.

Chemical changes involve a **chemical reaction** and do produce new substances. When iron rusts, iron oxide is formed, indicating a chemical change. Other examples of chemical changes include baking a cake, burning wood, digesting food, and mixing an acid and a base.

LAW OF CONSERVATION OF ENERGY

The **law of conservation of energy** states that in a closed system, energy cannot be created or destroyed but only changed from one form to another. This is also known as the first law of thermodynamics. Another way to state this is that the **total energy in an isolated system is constant**. Energy comes in many forms that may be transformed from one kind to another, but in a closed system, the total amount of energy is conserved or remains constant. For example, potential energy can be converted to kinetic energy, thermal energy, radiant energy, or mechanical energy. In an isolated chemical reaction, there can be no energy created or destroyed. The energy simply changes forms.

LAW OF CONSERVATION OF MASS

The **law of conservation of mass** is also known as the **law of conservation of matter**. This basically means that in a closed system, the total mass of the products must equal the total mass of the reactants. This could also be stated that in a closed system, mass never changes. A consequence of this law is that matter is never created or destroyed during a typical chemical reaction. The atoms of the reactants are simply rearranged to form the products. The number and type of each specific atom involved in the reactants is identical to the number and type of atoms in the products. This is the key principle used when balancing chemical equations. In a balanced chemical equation, the number of moles of each element on the reactant side equals the number of moles of each element on the product side.

> **Review Video: How Do You Balance Chemical Equations?**
> Visit mometrix.com/academy and enter code: 341228

CONVERSION OF ENERGY WITHIN CHEMICAL SYSTEMS

Chemical energy is the energy stored in molecules in the bonds between the atoms of those molecules and the energy associated with the intermolecular forces. This stored **potential energy** may be converted into **kinetic energy** and then into heat. During a chemical reaction, atoms may be rearranged and chemical bonds may be formed or broken accompanied by a corresponding absorption or release of energy, usually in the form of heat. According to the first law of thermodynamics, during these energy conversions, the **total amount of energy must be conserved**.

BONDS

Chemical bonds are the attractive forces that bind atoms together into molecules. Atoms form chemical bonds in an attempt to satisfy the octet rule. These bond types include covalent bonds, ionic bonds, and metallic bonds. **Covalent bonds** are formed from the sharing of electron pairs between two atoms in a molecule. **Ionic bonds** are formed from the transferring of electrons between one atom and another, which results in the formations of cations and anions. **Metallic bonding** results from the sharing of delocalized electrons among all of the atoms in a molecule.

IONIC BONDING

Ionic bonding results from the transfer of electrons between atoms. A **cation** or positive ion is formed when an atom loses one or more electrons. An **anion** or negative ion is formed when an atom gains one or more electrons. An ionic bond results from the electrostatic attraction between a cation and an anion. One example of a compound formed by ionic bonds is sodium chloride or NaCl. Sodium (Na) is an alkali metal and tends to form Na^+ ions. Chlorine (Cl) is a halogen and tends to form Cl^- ions. The Na^+ ion and the Cl^- ion are attracted to each other. This electrostatic attraction between these oppositely charged ions is what results in the ionic bond between them.

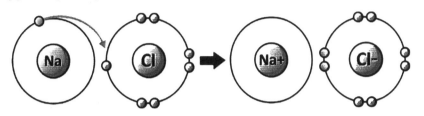

Review Video: Ionic Bonds
Visit mometrix.com/academy and enter code: 116546

COVALENT BONDING

Covalent bonding results from the sharing of electrons between atoms. Atoms seek to fill their valence shell and will share electrons with another atom in order to have a full octet (except hydrogen and helium, which only hold two electrons in their valence shells). **Molecular compounds** have covalent bonds. **Organic compounds** such as proteins, carbohydrates, lipids, and nucleic acids are molecular compounds formed by covalent bonds. Methane (CH_4) is a molecular compound in which one carbon atom is covalently bonded to four hydrogen atoms as shown below.

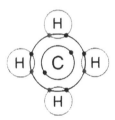

POLAR COVALENT BONDS, NONPOLAR COVALENT BONDS, AND HYBRIDIZATION

Polar covalent bonds result when electrons are shared unequally between atoms. **Nonpolar covalent bonds** result when electrons are shared equally between atoms. The unequal sharing of electrons is due to the differences in the electronegativities of the two atoms sharing the electrons. Partial charges develop due to this unequal sharing of electrons. The greater the difference in electronegativities between the two atoms, the stronger the dipole is. For example, the covalent bonds formed between the carbon atom and the two oxygen atoms in carbon dioxide are polar covalent bonds because the electronegativities of carbon and oxygen differ slightly. If the electronegativities are equal, then the covalent bonds are nonpolar. For example, the covalent double bond between two oxygen atoms is nonpolar because the oxygen atoms have the same electronegativities.

Review Video: Nonpolar Covalent Bonds
Visit mometrix.com/academy and enter code: 986465

Review Video: What are Covalent Bonds
Visit mometrix.com/academy and enter code: 482899

METALLIC BONDING

Metallic bonding is a type of bonding between metals. Metallic bonds are similar to covalent bonds in that they are a type of sharing of electrons between atoms. However, in covalent bonding, the electrons are shared with only one other atom. In metallic bonding, the electrons are shared with all the surrounding atoms. These electrons are referred to as delocalized electrons. Metallic bonding is responsible for many of the characteristics in metals including conductivity, malleability, and ductility. An example of metallic bonding is the metallic bond between the copper atoms in a piece of copper wire.

Review Video: Metallic Bonds
Visit mometrix.com/academy and enter code: 230855

GROUPS AND PERIODS IN THE PERIODIC TABLE

A **group** is a vertical column of the periodic table. Elements in the same group have the same number of **valence electrons**. For the representative elements, the number of valence electrons is equal to the group number. Because of their equal valence electrons, elements in the same groups have similar physical and chemical properties. A period is a horizontal row of the periodic table. Atomic number increases from left to right across a row. The **period** of an element corresponds to the **highest energy level** of the electrons in the atoms of that element. The energy level increases from top to bottom down a group.

Group →	1	2	3	4	5	6	7	8	9	10	11	12	13	14	15	16	17	18
Period 1	1 H																	2 He
2	3 Li	4 Be											5 B	6 C	7 N	8 O	9 F	10 Ne
3	11 Na	12 Mg											13 Al	14 Si	15 P	16 S	17 Cl	18 Ar
4	19 K	20 Ca	21 Sc	22 Ti	23 V	24 Cr	25 Mn	26 Fe	27 Co	28 Ni	29 Cu	30 Zn	31 Ga	32 Ge	33 As	34 Se	35 Br	36 Kr
5	37 Rb	38 Sr	39 Y	40 Zr	41 Nb	42 Mo	43 Tc	44 Ru	45 Rh	46 Pd	47 Ag	48 Cd	49 In	50 Sn	51 Sb	52 Te	53 I	54 Xe
6	55 Cs	56 Ba	*	72 Hf	73 Ta	74 W	75 Re	76 Os	77 Ir	78 Pt	79 Au	80 Hg	81 Tl	82 Pb	83 Bi	84 Po	85 At	86 Rn
7	87 Fr	88 Ra	**	104 Rf	105 Db	106 Sg	107 Bh	108 Hs	109 Mt	110 Ds	111 Rg	112 Cn	113 Uut	114 Fl	115 Uup	116 Lv	117 Uus	118 Uuo

	57 La	58 Ce	59 Pr	60 Nd	61 Pm	62 Sm	63 Eu	64 Gd	65 Tb	66 Dy	67 Ho	68 Er	69 Tm	70 Yb	71 Lu
*															
**	89 Ac	90 Th	91 Pa	92 U	93 Np	94 Pu	95 Am	96 Cm	97 Bk	98 Cf	99 Es	100 Fm	101 Md	102 No	103 Lr

Review Video: Periodic Table
Visit mometrix.com/academy and enter code: 154828

ATOMIC NUMBER AND ATOMIC MASS IN THE PERIODIC TABLE

The elements in the periodic table are arranged in order of **increasing atomic number** first left to right and then top to bottom across the periodic table. The **atomic number** represents the number of protons in the atoms of that element. Because of the increasing numbers of protons, the atomic mass typically also increases from left to right across a period and from top to bottom down a row. The **atomic mass** is a weighted average of all the naturally occurring isotopes of an element.

ATOMIC SYMBOLS

The **atomic symbol** for many elements is simply the first letter of the element name. For example, the atomic symbol for hydrogen is H, and the atomic symbol for carbon is C. The atomic symbol of other elements is the first two letters of the element name. For example, the atomic symbol for helium is He, and the atomic symbol for cobalt is Co. The atomic symbols of several elements are derived from Latin. For example, the atomic symbol for copper (Cu) is derived from *cuprum,* and the atomic symbol for iron (Fe) is derived from *ferrum.* The atomic symbol for tungsten (W) is derived from the German word *wolfram.*

ARRANGEMENT OF METALS, NONMETALS, AND METALLOIDS IN THE PERIODIC TABLE

The **metals** are located on the left side and center of the periodic table, and the **nonmetals** are located on the right side of the periodic table. The **metalloids** or **semimetals** form a zigzag line between the metals and nonmetals as shown below. Metals include the alkali metals such as lithium, sodium, and potassium and the alkaline earth metals such as beryllium, magnesium, and calcium. Metals also include the transition metals such as iron, copper, and nickel and the inner

37

transition metals such as thorium, uranium, and plutonium. Nonmetals include the chalcogens such as oxygen and sulfur, the halogens such as fluorine and chlorine, and the noble gases such as helium and argon. Carbon, nitrogen, and phosphorus are also nonmetals. Metalloids or semimetals include boron, silicon, germanium, antimony, and polonium.

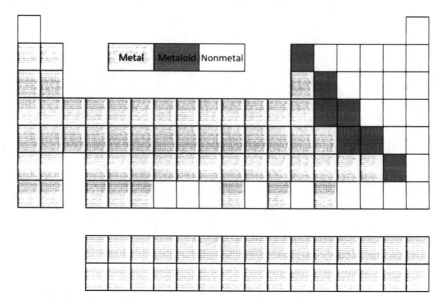

ARRANGEMENT OF TRANSITION ELEMENTS

The **transition elements** belong to one of two categories—transition metals or inner transition metals. The **transition metals** are located in the middle of the periodic table, and the inner transition metals are typically set off as two rows by themselves at the bottom of the periodic table. The transition metals correspond to the "d block" for orbital filling, and the inner transition metals correspond to the "f block" for orbital filling. Examples of transition metals include iron, copper, nickel, and zinc. The inner transition metals consist of the *lanthanide* or *rare-earth series*, which corresponds to the first row, and the *actinide series*, which corresponds to the second row of the inner transition metals. The *lanthanide series* includes lanthanum, cerium, and praseodymium. The *actinide series* includes actinium, uranium, and plutonium.

TYPES OF REACTIONS

One way to organize chemical reactions is to sort them into two categories: **oxidation/reduction reactions** (also called redox reactions) and **metathesis reactions** (which include acid/base reactions). Oxidation/reduction reactions can involve the transfer of one or more electrons, or they can occur as a result of the transfer of oxygen, hydrogen, or halogen atoms. The species that loses electrons is oxidized and is referred to as the reducing agent. The species that gains electrons is reduced and is referred to as the oxidizing agent. The element undergoing oxidation experiences an increase in its oxidation number, while the element undergoing reduction experiences a decrease in its oxidation number. **Single replacement reactions** are types of oxidation/reduction reactions. In a single replacement reaction, electrons are transferred from one chemical species to another. The transfer of electrons results in changes in the nature and charge of the species.

Review Video: Understanding Chemical Reactions
Visit mometrix.com/academy and enter code: 579876

Review Video: What is the Process of a Reaction?
Visit mometrix.com/academy and enter code: 808039

SINGLE SUBSTITUTION, DISPLACEMENT, AND REPLACEMENT REACTIONS

Single substitution, **displacement**, or **replacement reactions** are when one reactant is displaced by another to form the final product (A + BC → AB + C). Single substitution reactions can be cationic or anionic. When a piece of copper (Cu) is placed into a solution of silver nitrate ($AgNO_3$), the solution turns blue. The copper appears to be replaced with a silvery-white material. The equation is $2AgNO_3 + Cu → Cu(NO_3)_2 + 2Ag$. When this reaction takes place, the copper dissolves and the silver in the silver nitrate solution precipitates (becomes a solid), resulting in copper nitrate and silver. Copper and silver have switched places in the nitrate.

Double displacement, **double replacement**, **substitution**, **metathesis**, or **ion exchange reactions** are when ions or bonds are exchanged by two compounds to form different compounds (AC + BD → AD + BC). An example of this is that silver nitrate and sodium chloride form two different products (silver chloride and sodium nitrate) when they react. The formula for this reaction is $AgNO_3 + NaCl → AgCl + NaNO_3$.

> **Review Video: Single-Replacement Reactions**
> Visit mometrix.com/academy and enter code: 442975

COMBINATION AND DECOMPOSITION REACTIONS

Combination, or **synthesis**, **reactions**: In a combination reaction, two or more reactants combine to form a single product (A + B → AB). These reactions are also called synthesis or **addition reactions**. An example is burning hydrogen in air to produce water. The equation is $2H_2(g) + O_2(g) → 2H_2O(l)$. Another example is when water and sulfur trioxide react to form sulfuric acid. The equation is $H_2O + SO_3 → H_2SO_4$.

Decomposition (or desynthesis, decombination, or deconstruction) reactions: In a decomposition reaction, a reactant is broken down into two or more products (AB → A + B). These reactions are also called analysis reactions. **Thermal decomposition** is caused by heat. **Electrolytic decomposition** is due to electricity. An example of this type of reaction is the decomposition of water into hydrogen and oxygen gas. The equation is $2H_2O → 2H_2 + O_2$.

ACID/BASE REACTIONS

In **acid/base reactions**, an **acid** is a compound that can donate a proton, while a **base** is a compound that can accept a proton. In these types of reactions, the acid and base react to form a salt and water. When the proton is donated, the base becomes water and the remaining ions form a salt. One method of determining whether a reaction is an oxidation/reduction or a metathesis reaction is that the oxidation number of atoms does not change during a metathesis reaction.

ISOMERIZATION AND NEUTRALIZATION REACTIONS

Isomerization, or **rearrangement**, is the process of forming a compound's isomer. Within a compound, bonds are reformed. The reactant and product have the same molecular formula, but different structural formulas and different properties (A → B or A → A'). For example, butane (C_4H_{10}) is a hydrocarbon consisting of four carbon atoms in a straight chain. Heating it to 100° C or higher in the presence of a catalyst forms isobutane (methylpropane), which has a branched-chain structure. Boiling and freezing points are greatly different for butane and isobutane. A rearrangement reaction occurs within the molecule.

A **neutralization**, **acid-base**, or **proton transfer reaction** is when one compound acquires H^+ from another. These types of reactions are also usually double displacement reactions. The acid has an H^+ that is transferred to the base and neutralized to form a salt.

CHEMICAL KINETICS

Chemical kinetics is the study of the **rates** or speeds of **chemical reactions** and the various factors that affect these rates or speeds. The rate or speed of a reaction is the change in concentration of the reactants or products per unit of time. Another way to state this is that chemical kinetics is the study of the rate of change of the concentrations of the reactants and products and the factors that affect that rate of change. The study of catalysts is part of chemical kinetics. Catalysts are substances that speed up the rate of reactions without being consumed. Examples of reactions that occur at different rates include the explosion of trinitrotoluene (TNT), which occurs at a very fast rate, compared to the burning of a log, which occurs at a much slower rate.

Give the Rate Law for this General Reaction: $aA + bB + cC \rightarrow$ Products. Define Each Letter.

The rate of a chemical reaction can be defined as the following:

$$\text{rate} = \frac{\text{change in concentration}}{\text{change in time}}$$

This is usually represented by a rate law. The rate law for the general reaction $aA + bB + cC \rightarrow$ Products is given by rate $= k[A]^x[B]^y[C]^z$, where k is the rate constant; [A], [B], and [C] represent the concentrations of the reactants; and x, y, and z represent the reaction orders. The exponents x, y, and z must be experimentally determined. They do not necessarily equal the coefficients from the balanced chemical equation.

ACTIVATION ENERGY

Activation energy is the minimum amount of energy that must be possessed by reactant atoms or molecules in order to react. This is due to the fact that it takes a certain amount of energy to break bonds or form bonds between atoms. Reactants lacking the activation energy required will not be able to perform the necessary breaking or forming of bonds regardless of how often they collide. Catalysts lower the activation energy of a reaction and therefore increase the rate of reaction.

REACTION MECHANISM

Often, when studying specific reactions, only the net reactions are given. Realistically, reactions take place in a series of steps or elementary reactions as shown in the reaction mechanism. **Reaction mechanisms** show how a reaction proceeds in a **series of steps**. Some steps are slow, and some are fast. Each step has its own reaction mechanism. The slowest step in the reaction mechanism coincides with the step with the greatest activation energy. This step is known as the rate-determining step.

CATALYST

A **catalyst** is a chemical that **accelerates** or speeds up a chemical reaction without being consumed or used up in the reaction. Although catalysts are not consumed or permanently changed during the process of the reaction, catalysts do participate in the elementary reaction of the reaction mechanisms. Catalysts cannot make an impossible reaction take place, but catalysts do greatly increase the rate of a reaction. Catalysts lower the **activation energy**. Because the activation energy is the minimum energy required for molecules to react, lowering the activation energy makes it possible for more of the reactant molecules to react.

> **Review Video: Catalysts**
> Visit mometrix.com/academy and enter code: 288189

FACTORS THAT AFFECT REACTION RATE

Factors that affect reaction rate include concentration, surface area, and temperature. Increasing the **concentration** of the reactants increases the number of collisions between those reactants and therefore increases the reaction rate. Increasing the **surface area of contact** between the reactants also increases the number of collisions and therefore increases the reaction rate. Finally, increasing the **temperature** of the reactants increases the number of collisions but more significantly also increases the kinetic energy of the reactants, which in turn increases the fraction of molecules meeting the activation energy requirement. With more molecules at the activation energy, more of the reactants are capable of completing the reaction.

DILUTE AND CONCENTRATED

The terms **dilute** and **concentrated** have opposite meanings. In a solution, the **solute** is dissolved in the **solvent**. The more solute that is dissolved, the more concentrated is the solution. The less solute that is dissolved, the less concentrated and the more dilute is the solution. The terms are often associated with the preparation of a stock solution for a laboratory experiment. Stock solutions are typically ordered in a concentrated solution. To prepare for use in a chemistry lab, the stock solutions are diluted to the appropriate molarity by adding a specific amount of solvent such as water to a specific amount of stock solution.

SATURATED, UNSATURATED, AND SUPERSATURATED

The terms *saturated, unsaturated,* and *supersaturated* are associated with solutions. In a **solution**, a **solute** is added to a **solvent**. In a saturated solution, the solute is added to the solvent until no more solute is able to dissolve. The undissolved solute will settle down to the bottom of the beaker. A solution is considered unsaturated as long as more solute is able to go into solution under ordinary conditions. The solubility of solids in liquids typically increases as temperature increases. If the temperature of a solution is increased as the solute is being added, more solute than is normally possible may go into solution, forming a supersaturated solution.

MIXTURE, SOLUTION, AND COLLOID

A **mixture** is made of two or more substances that are combined in various proportions. The exact proportion of the constituents is the defining characteristic of any mixture. There are two types of mixtures: homogeneous and heterogeneous. **Homogeneous** means that the mixture's composition and properties are uniform throughout. Conversely, **heterogeneous** means that the mixture's composition and properties are not uniform throughout.

A **solution** is a homogeneous mixture of substances that cannot be separated by filtration or centrifugation. Solutions are made by dissolving one or more solutes into a solvent. For example, in an aqueous glucose solution, glucose is the solute and water is the solvent. If there is more than one liquid present in the solution, then the most prevalent liquid is considered the solvent. The exact mechanism of dissolving varies depending on the mixture, but the result is always individual solute ions or molecules surrounded by solvent molecules. The proportion of solute to solvent for a particular solution is its **concentration**.

A **colloid** is a heterogeneous mixture in which small particles (<1 micrometer) are suspended, but not dissolved, in a liquid. As such, they can be separated by centrifugation. A commonplace example of a colloid is milk.

> **Review Video: Solutions**
> Visit mometrix.com/academy and enter code: 995937

EFFECTS OF TEMPERATURE, SURFACE AREA, AGITATION, AND PRESSURE ON THE DISSOLUTION RATE

Temperature, pressure, surface area, and agitation affect the **dissolution rate**. Increasing the **temperature** increases the kinetic energy of the molecules, which increases the number of collisions with the solute particles. Increasing the **surface area** of contact by stirring (agitation) or crushing a solid solute also increases the dissolution rate and helps prevent recrystallization. Increasing the **pressure** will increase the dissolution rate for gas solutes in liquid solvents because the added pressure will make it more difficult for the gas to escape. Increasing the pressure will have virtually no effect on the dissolution rate for solid solutes in liquid solvents under normal conditions.

EFFECT OF TEMPERATURE AND PRESSURE ON SOLUBILITY

Temperature and pressure affect **solubility**. For gas solutes in liquid solvents, increasing the **temperature** increases the kinetic energy causing more gas particles to escape the surface of the liquid solvents and therefore decreasing the solubility of the solutes. For most solid solutes in liquid solvents, increasing the temperature increases the solubility, as shown in this solubility curve for selected salts. For gas solutes in liquid solvents, increasing the **pressure** increases the solubility. Increasing the pressure of liquid or solid solutes in liquid solvents has virtually no effect under normal conditions.

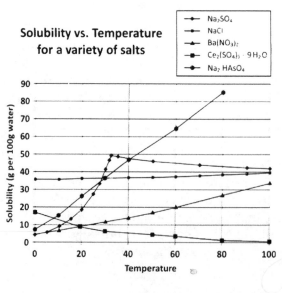

42

DIFFERENCES BETWEEN ACIDS AND BASES

There are several differences between **acids** and **bases**. Acidic solutions tend to taste sour, whereas basic solutions tend to taste bitter. Dilute bases tend to feel slippery, whereas dilute acids feel like water. Active metals such as magnesium and zinc react with acids to produce hydrogen gas, but active metals usually do not react with bases. Acids and bases form electrolytes in aqueous solutions and conduct electricity. Acids turn blue litmus red, but bases turn red litmus blue. Acidic solutions have a pH of less than 7, whereas basic solutions have a pH of greater than 7.

> **Review Video: Properties of Acids and Bases**
> Visit mometrix.com/academy and enter code: 645283

ARRHENIUS ACID AND BASE

Arrhenius acids are substances that produce hydrogen ions (H^+) when dissolved in water to form aqueous solutions. Arrhenius bases are substances that produce hydroxide ions (OH^-) when dissolved in water to form aqueous solutions. The **Arrhenius concept** is limited to acids and bases in aqueous solutions and cannot be applied to other solids, liquids, and gases. Examples of Arrhenius acids include hydrochloric acid (HCl) and sulfuric acid (H_2SO_4). Examples of Arrhenius bases include sodium hydroxide (NaOH) and magnesium hydroxide ($Mg(OH)_2$).

BRØNSTED–LOWRY ACID AND BASE

The Brønsted–Lowry concept is based on the donation or the acceptance of a proton. According to the **Brønsted–Lowry concept**, an acid is a substance that donates one or more protons to another substance and a base is a substance that accepts a proton from another substance. The Brønsted–Lowry concept can be applied to substances other than aqueous solutions. This concept is much broader than the Arrhenius concept, which can only be applied to aqueous solutions. The Brønsted–Lowry concept states that a substance cannot act like an acid (donate its proton) unless another substance is available to act as a base (accept the donated proton). In this concept, water may act as either an acid or a base. Hydrochloric acid (HCl) is an example of a Brønsted–Lowry acid. Ammonia (NH_3) is an example of a Brønsted–Lowry base.

LEWIS ACID AND BASE

A **Lewis acid** is any substance that can accept a pair of nonbonding electrons. A **Lewis base** is any substance that can donate a pair of nonbonding electrons. According to the **Lewis theory**, all cations such as Mg^{2+} and Cu^{2+} are Lewis acids. Trigonal planar molecules, which are exceptions to the octet rule such as BF_3, are Lewis acids. Molecules such as CO_2 that have multiple bonds between two atoms that differ in electronegativities are Lewis acids, also. According to the Lewis theory, all anions such as OH^- are Lewis bases. Other examples of Lewis bases include trigonal pyramidal molecules such as ammonia, NH_3, and nonmetal oxides such as carbon monoxide, CO. Some compounds such as water, H_2O, can be either Lewis acids or bases.

NEUTRALIZATION REACTION

Neutralization is a reaction of an acid and a base that yields a salt and water. The general form of the reaction is:

$$\text{acid} + \text{base} \rightarrow \text{salt} + \text{water}$$

The salt is formed from the cation of the base and the anion of the acid. The water is formed from the cation of the acid and the anion of the base.

An example is the neutralization reaction of hydrochloric acid and sodium hydroxide to form sodium chloride and water:

$$HCl(aq) + NaOH(aq) \rightarrow NaCl(s) + H_2O(l)$$

EQUIVALENCE POINT

The **equivalence point** is by definition the point in a titration at which the analyte is neutralized. When the acid–base indicator starts to change color, the equivalence point has been reached. At this point, equivalent amounts of acids and bases have reacted. Also, at this point, $[H^+] = [OH^-]$. On an acid–base titration curve, the slope of the curve increases dramatically at the equivalence point. For strong acids and bases, the equivalence point occurs at a pH of 7. The figures below show the equivalence points for a strong acid titrated with a strong base (a) and a strong base titrated with a strong acid (b).

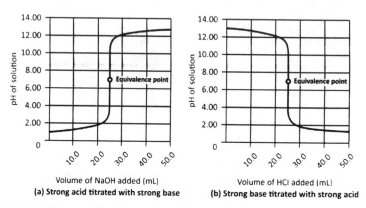

(a) Strong acid titrated with strong base

(b) Strong base titrated with strong acid

Review Video: Titration
Visit mometrix.com/academy and enter code: 550131

Biology

BIOCHEMICAL PATHWAYS

Autotrophs that use light to produce energy use **photosynthesis** as a biochemical pathway. In eukaryotic autotrophs photosynthesis takes place in chloroplasts. Prokaryotic autotrophs that use inorganic chemical reactions to produce energy use **chemosynthesis** as a biochemical pathway. Heterotrophs require food and use **cellular respiration** to release energy from chemical bonds in the food. All organisms use cellular respiration to release energy from stored food. Cellular respiration can be aerobic or anaerobic. Most eukaryotes use cellular respiration that takes place in the mitochondria.

PHOTOSYNTHESIS

Photosynthesis is a food-making process that occurs in three processes: light-capturing events, light-dependent reactions, and light-independent reactions. In light-capturing events, the thylakoids of the chloroplasts, which contain chlorophyll and accessory pigments, absorb light energy and produce excited electrons. Thylakoids also contain enzymes and electron-transport molecules. Molecules involved in this process are arranged in groups called photosystems. In light-dependent reactions, the excited electrons from the light-capturing events are moved by electron transport in a series of steps in which they are used to split water into hydrogen and oxygen ions. The oxygen is released, and the NADP+ bonds with the hydrogen atoms and forms NADPH. ATP is

44

produced from the excited elections. The light-independent reactions use this ATP, NADPH, and carbon dioxide to produce sugars.

C_3 AND C_4 PHOTOSYNTHESIS

Plants undergo an additional process during photosynthesis that is known as photorespiration. Photorespiration is a wasteful process that uses energy and decreases sugar synthesis. This process occurs when the enzyme rubisco binds to oxygen rather than atmospheric carbon dioxide. There are three different processes that plants use to fix carbon during photosynthesis and these include C_3, C_4, and crassulacean acid metabolism (CAM). Some plants, such as C_4 and CAM plants, can decrease photorespiration and therefore minimize energy lost while C_3 plants, which make up more than 85% of plants, have no special adaptations to stop photorespiration from occuring. C_3 and C_4 plants are named for the type of carbon molecule (three-carbon or four-carbon) that is made during the first step of the reaction. The first step of the C_3 process involves the formation of two three-carbon molecules (3-phosphoglycerate; 3-PGA) from carbon dioxide being fixed by the enzyme. The first step of C_4 photosynthesis is carbon dioxide beign fixed by the enzyme PEP carboxylase, which unlike rubisco does not have the ability to bind to oxygen. This fixation forms a four-carbon molecule (oxaloaceate) and these initial steps occur in the mesophyll cell. Next, oxaloacetate is converted into a malate, a molecule that can enter the bundle sheath cells, and then is broken down to release carbon dioxide. From there, the carbon dioxide is fixed by rubisco as it undergoes the Calvin cycle seen in C_3 photosynthesis. Because C_4 plants undergo an initial step that allows carbon dioxide to be more readily available, with the use of malate, photorespiration is minimized.

CRASSULACEAN ACID METABOLISM

Crassulacean acid metabolism (CAM) is a form of photosynthesis adapted to dry environments. While C_4 plants separate the Calvin cycle via space, or by having different cells for different functions and processes, CAM plants separate the processes by time of day. During the night, pores of the plant leaves, called stomata, open to receive carbon dioxide, which combines with PEP carboxylase to form oxaloacetate. Oxaloacetate is eventually converted into malate, which is stored in vacuoles until the next day. During the following day, the stomata are closed and the malate is transported to chloroplasts, where malate is broken down into pyruvate (three-carbon molecule) and carbon dioxide. The carbon dioxide released from malate is used in photosynthesis during the daytime. One advantage of the CAM cycle is that it minimizes loss of water through the stomata during the daytime. A second advantage is that concentrating carbon dioxide in the chloroplasts in this manner increases the efficiency of the enzyme rubisco to fix carbon dioxide and complete the Calvin cycle.

AEROBIC RESPIRATION

Aerobic cellular respiration is a series of enzyme-controlled chemical reactions in which oxygen reacts with glucose to produce carbon dioxide and water, releasing energy in the form of adenosine triphosphate (ATP). Cellular respiration occurs in a series of three processes: glycolysis, the Krebs cycle, and the electron-transport system.

GLYCOLYSIS

Glycolysis is a series of enzyme-controlled chemical reactions that occur in the cell's cytoplasm. Each glucose molecule is split in half to produce two pyruvic acid molecules, four ATP molecules, and two NADH molecules. Because two ATP molecules are used to split the glucose molecule, the net ATP yield for glycolysis is two ATP molecules.

> **Review Video: Glycolysis**
> Visit mometrix.com/academy and enter code: 466815

KREBS CYCLE

The **Krebs cycle** is also called the citric acid cycle or the tricarboxylic acid cycle (TCA). It is a **catabolic pathway** in which the bonds of glucose and occasionally fats or lipids are broken down and reformed into ATP. It is a respiration process that uses oxygen and produces carbon dioxide, water, and ATP. Cells require energy from ATP to synthesize proteins from amino acids and replicate DNA. The cycle is acetyl CoA, citric acid, isocitric acid, ketoglutaric acid (products are amino acids and CO_2), succinyl CoA, succinic acid, fumaric acid, malic acid, and oxaloacetic acid. One of the products of the Krebs cycle is NADH, which is then used in the electron chain transport system to manufacture ATP. From glycolysis, pyruvate is oxidized in a step linking to the Krebs cycle. After the Krebs cycle, NADH and succinate are oxidized in the electron transport chain.

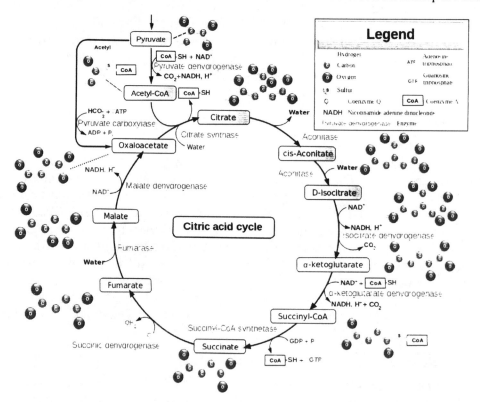

ELECTRON TRANSPORT CHAIN

The **electron transport chain** is part of phosphorylation, whereby electrons are transported from enzyme to enzyme until they reach a final acceptor. The electron transport chain includes a series of oxidizing and reducing molecules involved in the release of energy. In **redox reactions**, electrons are removed from a substrate (oxidative) and H^+ (protons) can also be simultaneously removed. A substrate gains electrons during reduction. For example, when glucose is oxidized, electrons are lost and energy is released. There are enzymes in the membranes of mitochondria. The electrons are carried from one enzyme to another by a co-enzyme. Protons are also released to the other side of the membrane. For example, FAD and $FADH_2$ are used in oxidative phosphorylation. FAD is reduced to $FADH_2$. Electrons are stored there and then sent onward, and the $FADH_2$ becomes FAD again. In aerobic respiration, the final electron acceptor is O_2. In anaerobic respiration, it is something other than O_2.

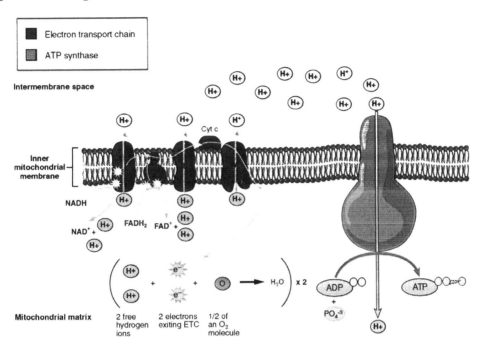

FERMENTATION

Fermentation is an anaerobic reaction in which glucose is only partially broken down. It releases energy through the oxidation of sugars or other types of organic molecules. Oxygen is sometimes involved, but not always. It is different from respiration in that it uses neither the Krebs cycle nor the electron transport chain and the final electron acceptor is an organic molecule. It uses **substrate-level phosphorylation** to form ATP. NAD^+ is reduced to NADH and NADH further reduces pyruvic acid to various end products. Fermentation can lead to excess waste products and is less efficient than aerobic respiration. **Homolactic fermentation** refers to lactic acid fermentation in which the sugars are converted to lactic acid only (there is one end product). In **heterolactic fermentation**, the sugars are converted to a range of products.

EXAMPLES OF FERMENTATION

Lactic acid fermentation is the breakdown of glucose and six-carbon sugars into lactic acid to release energy. It is an anaerobic process, meaning that it does not require oxygen. It can occur in muscle cells and is also performed by streptococcus and lactobacillus bacteria. It can also be used to making yogurt and other food products.

Alcohol fermentation is the breakdown of glucose and six-carbon sugars into ethanol and carbon dioxide to release energy. It is an anaerobic process. It is performed by yeast and used in the production of alcoholic beverages.

CHEMOSYNTHESIS

Chemosynthesis is the food-making process of chemoautotrophs in extreme environments such as deep-sea-vents, or hydrothermal vents. Unlike photosynthesis, chemosynthesis does not require light. In general, chemosynthesis involves the oxidation of inorganic substances to make a sugar, but there are several species that use different pathways or processses. For example, sulfur bacteria live near or in deep-sea vents and oxidize hydrogen sulfide released from those vents to make a sugar. Instead of sunlight, chemosynthesis uses the energy stored in the chemical bonds of chemicals such as hydrogen sulfide to produce food. During chemosynthesis, the electrons that are removed from the inorganic molecules are combined with carbon dioxide and oxygen to produce sugar, sulfur, and water. Some bacteria use metal ions such as iron and magnesium to obtain the needed electrons. For example, methanobacteria such as those found in human intestines combine carbon dioxide and hydrogen gas and release methane as a waste product. Nitrogen bacteria such as nitrogen-fixing bacteria in the nodules of legumes convert atmospheric nitrogen into nitrates.

PROKARYOTES AND EUKARYOTES

SIZES AND METABOLISM

Cells of the domains of Bacteria and Archaea are **prokaryotes**. Bacteria cells and Archaea cells are much smaller than cells of eukaryotes. Prokaryote cells are usually only 1 to 2 micrometers in diameter, but eukaryotic cells are usually at least 10 times and possibly 100 times larger than prokaryotic cells. Eukaryotic cells are usually 10 to 100 micrometers in diameter. Most prokaryotes are unicellular organisms, although some prokaryotes live in colonies. Because of their large surface-area-to-volume ratios, prokaryotes have a very high metabolic rate. **Eukaryotic cells** are much larger than prokaryotic cells. Due to their larger sizes, they have a much smaller surface-area-to-volume ratio and consequently have much lower metabolic rates.

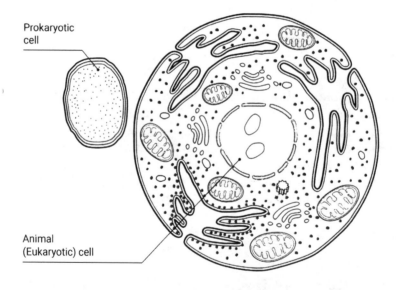

Prokaryotic cell

Animal (Eukaryotic) cell

Review Video: <u>Prokaryotic and Eukaryotic Cells</u>
Visit mometrix.com/academy and enter code: 231438
Review Video: <u>Cell Structure</u>
Visit mometrix.com/academy and enter code: 591293

MEMBRANE-BOUND ORGANELLES

Prokaryotic cells are much simpler than eukaryotic cells. Prokaryote cells do not have a nucleus due to their small size and their DNA is located in the center of the cell in a region referred to as a **nucleoid**. Eukaryote cells have a **nucleus** bound by a double membrane. Eukaryotic cells typically

have hundreds or thousands of additional **membrane-bound organelles** that are independent of the cell membrane. Prokaryotic cells do not have any membrane-bound organelles that are independent of the cell membrane. Once again, this is probably due to the much larger size of the eukaryotic cells. The organelles of eukaryotes give them much higher levels of intracellular division than is possible in prokaryotic cells.

CELL WALLS

Not all cells have cell walls, but most prokaryotes have cell walls. The cell walls of organisms from the domain Bacteria differ from the cell walls of the organisms from the domain Archaea. Some eukaryotes, such as some fungi, some algae, and plants, have cell walls that differ from the cell walls of the Bacteria and Archaea domains. The main difference between the cell walls of different domains or kingdoms is the composition of the cell walls. For example, most bacteria have cell walls outside of the plasma membrane that contains the molecule peptidoglycan. **Peptidoglycan** is a large polymer of amino acids and sugars. The peptidoglycan helps maintain the strength of the cell wall. Some of the Archaea cells have cell walls containing the molecule pseudopeptidoglycan, which differs in chemical structure from the peptidoglycan but basically provides the same strength to the cell wall. Some fungi cell walls contain **chitin**. The cell walls of diatoms, a type of yellow algae, contain silica. Plant cell walls contain cellulose, and woody plants are further strengthened by lignin. Some algae also contain lignin. Animal cells do not have cell walls.

CHROMOSOME STRUCTURE

Prokaryote cells have DNA arranged in a **circular structure** that should not be referred to as a chromosome. Due to the small size of a prokaryote cell, the DNA material is simply located near the center of the cell in a region called the nucleoid. A prokaryotic cell may also contain tiny rings of DNA called plasmids. Prokaryote cells lack histone proteins, and therefore the DNA is not actually packaged into chromosomes. Prokaryotes reproduce by binary fission, while eukaryotes reproduce by mitosis with the help of **linear chromosomes** and histone proteins. During mitosis, the chromatin is tightly wound on the histone proteins and packaged as a chromosome. The DNA in a eukaryotic cell is located in the membrane-bound nucleus.

> **Review Video: Chromosomes**
> Visit mometrix.com/academy and enter code: 132083

CELL CYCLE STAGES

The cell cycle consists of three stages: interphase, mitosis, and cytokinesis. **Interphase** is the longest stage of the cell cycle and involves the cell growing and making a copy of its DNA. Cells typically spend more than 90% of the cell cycle in interphase. Interphase includes two growth phases called G_1 and G_2. The order of interphase is the first growth cycle, **GAP 1** (G_1 phase), followed by the **synthesis phase** (S), and ending with the second growth phase, **GAP 2** (G_2 phase). During the G_1 phase of interphase, the cell increases the number of organelles by forming diploid cells. During the S phase of interphase, the DNA is replicated, and the chromosomes are doubled.

During the G_2 phase of interphase, the cell synthesizes needed proteins and organelles, continues to increase in size, and prepares for mitosis. Once the G_2 phase ends, mitosis can begin.

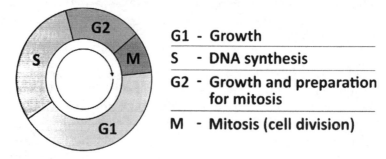

G1 - Growth

S - DNA synthesis

G2 - Growth and preparation for mitosis

M - Mitosis (cell division)

MITOSIS

Mitosis is the asexual process of cell division. During mitosis, one parent cell divides into two identical daughter cells. Mitosis is used for growth, repair, and replacement of cells. Some unicellular organisms reproduce asexually by mitosis. Some multicellular organisms can reproduce by fragmentation or budding, which involves mitosis. Mitosis consists of four phases: prophase, metaphase, anaphase, and telophase. During **prophase**, the spindle fibers appear, and the DNA is condensed and packaged as chromosomes that become visible. The nuclear membrane also breaks down, and the nucleolus disappears. During **metaphase**, the spindle apparatus is formed and the centromeres of the chromosomes line up on the equatorial plane. During **anaphase**, the centromeres divide and the two chromatids separate and are pulled toward the opposite poles of the cell. During **telophase**, the spindle fibers disappear, the nuclear membrane reforms, and the DNA in the chromatids is decondensed.

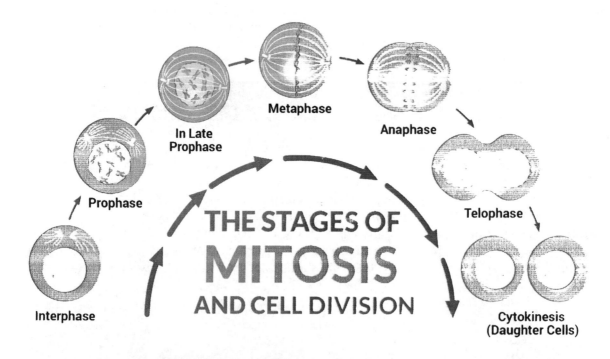

THE STAGES OF MITOSIS AND CELL DIVISION

Interphase

Prophase

In Late Prophase

Metaphase

Anaphase

Telophase

Cytokinesis (Daughter Cells)

Review Video: Mitosis
Visit mometrix.com/academy and enter code: 849894

CYTOKINESIS

Cytokinesis is the dividing of the cytoplasm and cell membrane by the pinching of a cell into two new daughter cells at the end of mitosis. This occurs at the end of telophase when the actin filaments in the cytoskeleton form a contractile ring that narrows and divides the cell. In plant cells, a cell plate forms across the phragmoplast, which is the center of the spindle apparatus. In animal cells, as the contractile ring narrows, the cleavage furrow forms. Eventually, the contractile ring narrows down to the spindle apparatus joining the two cells and the cells eventually divide. Diagrams of the cleavage furrow of an animal cell and cell plate of a plant are shown below.

Animal cell

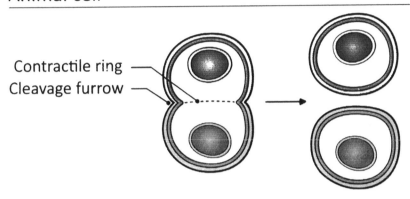

Plant cell

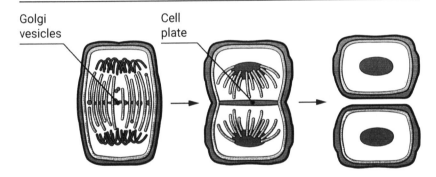

MEIOSIS

Meiosis is a type of cell division in which the number of chromosomes is reduced by half. Meiosis produces gametes, or egg and sperm cells. Meiosis occurs in two successive stages, which consist of a first mitotic division followed by a second mitotic division. During **meiosis I**, or the first meiotic division, the cell replicates its DNA in interphase and then continues through prophase I, metaphase I, anaphase I, and telophase I. At the end of meiosis I, there are two daughter cells that have the same number of chromosomes as the parent cell. During **meiosis II**, the cell enters a brief interphase but does not replicate its DNA. Then, the cell continues through prophase II, metaphase II, anaphase II, and telophase II. During prophase II, the unduplicated chromosomes split. At the end of telophase II, there are four daughter cells that have half the number of chromosomes as the parent cell.

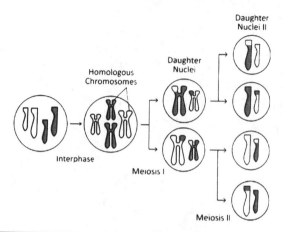

CELL CYCLE CHECKPOINTS

During the cell cycle, the cell goes through three checkpoints to ensure that the cell is dividing properly at each phase, that it is the appropriate time for division, and that the cell has not been damaged. The **first checkpoint** is at the end of the G_1 phase just before the cell undergoes the S phase, or synthesis. At this checkpoint, a cell may continue with cell division, delay the division, or rest. This **resting phase** is called G_0. In animal cells, the G_1 checkpoint is called **restriction**. Proteins called cyclin D and cyclin E, which are dependent on enzymes cyclin-dependent kinase 4 and cyclin-dependent kinase 2 (CDK4 and CDK2), respectively, largely control this first checkpoint. The **second checkpoint** is at the end of the G_2 phase just before the cell begins prophase during mitosis. The protein cyclin A, which is dependent on the enzyme CDK2, largely controls this checkpoint. During mitosis, the **third checkpoint** occurs at metaphase to check that the chromosomes are lined up along the equatorial plane. This checkpoint is largely controlled by cyclin B, which is dependent upon the enzyme CDK1.

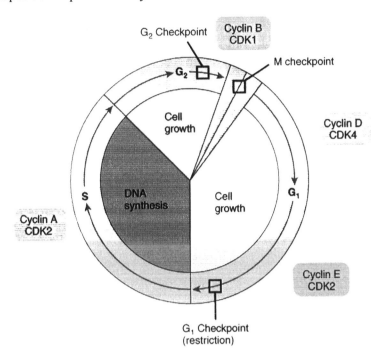

MUTATIONS

MISSENSE MUTATIONS, SILENT MUTATIONS, AND NONSENSE MUTATIONS

Mutations are changes in DNA sequences. **Point mutations** are changes in a single nucleotide in a DNA sequence. Three types of point mutations are missense, silent, and nonsense.

- **Missense mutations** result in a codon for a different amino acid. An example is mutating TGT (Cysteine codon) to TGG (Tryptophan codon).
- **Silent mutations** result in a codon for the same amino acid as the original sequence. An example is mutating TGT (Cysteine codon) to TGC (a different Cysteine codon).
- **Nonsense mutations** insert a premature stop codon, typically resulting in a non-functional protein. An example is mutating TGT (Cysteine codon) to TGA (STOP codon).

> **Review Video: Codons**
> Visit mometrix.com/academy and enter code: 978172

FRAMESHIFT MUTATIONS AND INVERSION MUTATIONS

Deletions and insertions can result in the addition of amino acids, the removal of amino acids, or cause a frameshift mutation. A **frameshift mutation** changes the reading frame of the mRNA (a new group of codons will be read), resulting in the formation of a new protein product. Mutations can also occur on the chromosomal level. For example, an **inversion** is when a piece of the chromosome inverts or flips its orientation.

GERMLINE MUTATIONS AND SOMATIC MUTATIONS

Mutations can occur in somatic (body) cells and germ cells (egg and sperm). **Somatic mutations** develop after conception and occur in an organism's body cells such as bone cells, liver cells, or brain cells. Somatic mutations cannot be passed on from parent to offspring. The mutation is limited to the specific descendent of the cell in which the mutation occurred. The mutation is not in the other body cells unless they are descendants of the originally mutated cell. Somatic mutations may cause cancer or diseases. Some somatic mutations are silent. **Germline mutations** are present at conception and occur in an organism's germ cells, which are only egg and sperms cells. Germline mutations may be passed on from parent to offspring. Germline mutations will be present in every cell of an offspring that inherits a germline mutation. Germline mutations may cause diseases. Some germline mutations are silent.

MUTAGENS

Mutagens are physical and chemical agents that cause changes or errors in DNA replication. Mutagens are external factors to an organism. Examples include ionizing radiation such as ultraviolet radiation, x-rays, and gamma radiation. Viruses and microorganisms that integrate their DNA into host chromosomes are also mutagens. Mutagens include environmental poisons such as asbestos, coal tars, tobacco, and benzene. Alcohol and diets high in fat have been shown to be mutagenic. Not all mutations are caused by mutagens. **Spontaneous mutations** can occur in DNA due to molecular decay.

LAW OF SEGREGATION

The **law of segregation** states that the alleles for a trait separate when gametes are formed, which means that only one of the pair of alleles for a given trait is passed to the gamete. This can be shown in monohybrid crosses, which can be used to show which allele is **dominant** for a single trait. A **monohybrid cross** is a genetic cross between two organisms with a different variation for a single trait. The first monohybrid cross typically occurs between two **homozygous** parents. Each parent is homozygous for a separate allele (gg or GG) for a particular trait. For example, in pea plants, green seeds (G) are dominant over yellow seeds(g). Therefore, in a genetic cross of two pea plants that are homozygous for seed color, the F_1 generation will be 100% **heterozygous** green seeds.

	g	g
G	Gg	Gg
G	Gg	Gg

Review Video: Punnett Square
Visit mometrix.com/academy and enter code: 853855

MONOHYBRID CROSS FOR A CROSS BETWEEN TWO Gg PARENTS

If the plants with the heterozygous green seeds are crossed, the F_2 generation should be 50% heterozygous green (Gg), 25% homozygous green (GG), and 25% homozygous yellow (gg).

	G	g
G	GG	Gg
g	Gg	gg

LAW OF INDEPENDENT ASSORTMENT

Mendel's law of independent assortment states that alleles of one characteristic or trait separate independently of the alleles of another characteristic. Therefore, the allele a gamete receives for one gene does not influence the allele received for another gene due to the allele pairs separating

54

independently during gamete formation. This means that traits are transmitted independently of each other. This can be shown in dihybrid crosses.

GENE, GENOTYPE, PHENOTYPE, AND ALLELE

A **gene** is a portion of DNA that identifies how traits are expressed and passed on in an organism. A gene is part of the genetic code. Collectively, all genes form the **genotype** of an individual. The genotype includes genes that may not be expressed, such as recessive genes. The **phenotype** is the physical, visual manifestation of genes. It is determined by the basic genetic information and how genes have been affected by their environment.

An **allele** is a variation of a gene. Also known as a trait, it determines the manifestation of a gene. This manifestation results in a specific physical appearance of some facet of an organism, such as eye color or height. The genetic information for eye color is a gene. The gene variations responsible for blue, green, brown, or black eyes are called alleles. **Locus** (pl. loci) refers to the location of a gene or alleles.

> **Review Video: Genotype vs Phenotype**
> Visit mometrix.com/academy and enter code: 922853

DOMINANT AND RECESSIVE GENES

Gene traits are represented in pairs with an uppercase letter for the **dominant trait** (A) and a lowercase letter for the **recessive trait** (a). Genes occur in pairs (AA, Aa, or aa). There is one gene on each chromosome half supplied by each parent organism. Since half the genetic material is from each parent, the offspring's traits are represented as a combination of these. A dominant trait only requires one gene of a gene pair for it to be expressed in a phenotype, whereas a recessive requires both genes in order to be manifested. For example, if the mother's genotype is Dd and the father's is dd, the possible combinations are Dd and dd. The dominant trait will be manifested if the genotype is DD or Dd. The recessive trait will be manifested if the genotype is dd. Both DD and dd are **homozygous** pairs. Dd is **heterozygous**.

DIHYBRID CROSS FOR THE F$_2$ GENERATION OF A CROSS BETWEEN GGRR AND ggrr PARENTS

A **dihybrid cross** is a genetic cross for two traits that each have two alleles. For example, in pea plants, green seeds (G) are dominant over yellow seeds (g), and round seeds (R) are dominant over wrinkled seeds (r). In a genetic cross of two pea plants that are homozygous for seed color and seed shape (GGRR or ggRR), the F$_1$ generation will be 100% heterozygous green and round seeds (GgRr). If these F$_1$ plants (GgRr) are crossed, the resulting F$_2$ generation is shown below. Out of the 16 total genotypes for the cross of green, round seeds, there are only four possible phenotypes, or physical traits of the seed: green and round seed (GGRR, GGRr, GgRR, or GgRr), green and wrinkled seed (GGrr or Ggrr), yellow and round seed (ggRR or ggRr) , or yellow and wrinkled seed (ggrr). There are nine green and round seed plants, three green and wrinkled seed plants, three yellow and round seed plants, and only one yellow and wrinkled seed plant. This cross has a **9:3:3:1 ratio**.

	GR	gR	Gr	gr
GR	GGRR	GgRR	GGRr	GgRr
gR	GgRR	ggRR	GgRr	ggRr
Gr	GGRr	GgRr	GGrr	Ggrr
gr	GgRr	ggRr	Ggrr	ggrr

PEDIGREE

Pedigree analysis is a type of genetic analysis in which an inherited trait is studied and traced through several generations of a family to determine how that trait is inherited. A pedigree is a chart arranged as a type of family tree using symbols for people and lines to represent the relationships between those people. Squares usually represent males, and circles represent females. **Horizontal lines** represent a male and female mating, and the **vertical lines** beneath them represent their children. Usually, family members who possess the trait are fully shaded and those that are carriers only of the trait are half-shaded. Genotypes and phenotypes are determined for each individual if possible. The pedigree below shows the family tree of a family in which the first male who was red-green color blind mated with the first female who was unaffected. They had five children. The three sons were unaffected, and the two daughters were carriers.

Inheritance of Red-Green Color Blindness:
an X-linked Recessive Trait

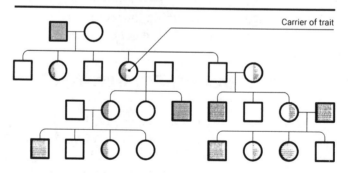

GENETIC DRIFT

Genetic drift is a microevolutionary process that causes random changes in allele frequencies that are not the result of natural selection. Genetic drift can result in a loss of genetic diversity. Genetic drift greatly impacts small populations. Two special forms of genetic drift are the genetic bottleneck and the founder effect. A **genetic bottleneck** occurs when there is a drastic reduction in population due to some change such as overhunting, disease, or habitat loss. When a population is greatly reduced in size, many alleles can be lost. Even if the population size greatly increases again, the lost alleles represent lost genetic diversity. The **founder effect** occurs when one individual or a few individuals populate a new area such as an island. This new population is limited to the alleles of the founder(s) unless mutations occur or new individuals immigrate to the region.

GENE FLOW

Gene flow is a microevolutionary process in which alleles enter a population by immigration and leave a population by emigration. Gene flow helps counter genetic drift. When individuals from one genetically distinct population immigrate to a different genetically distinct population, alleles and their genetic information are added to the new population. The added alleles will change the gene frequencies within the population. This increases genetic diversity. If individuals with rare alleles emigrate from a population, the genetic diversity is decreased. Gene flow reduces the genetic differences between populations.

MECHANISMS OF EVOLUTION

NATURAL AND ARTIFICIAL SELECTION

Natural selection and artificial selection are both mechanisms of evolution. **Natural selection** is a process of nature in which a population can change over generations. Every population has variations in individual heritable traits and organisms best suited for survival typically reproduce and pass on those genetic traits to offspring to increase the likelihood of them surviving. Typically, the more advantageous a trait is, the more common that trait becomes in a population. Natural selection brings about evolutionary **adaptations** and is responsible for biological diversity. Artificial selection is another mechanism of evolution. **Artificial selection** is a process brought about by humans. Artificial selection is the selective breeding of domesticated animals and plants such as when farmers choose animals or plants with desirable traits to reproduce. Artificial selection has led to the evolution of farm stock and crops. For example, cauliflower, broccoli, and cabbage all evolved due to artificial selection of the wild mustard plant.

SEXUAL SELECTION

Sexual selection is a special case of natural selection in animal populations. **Sexual selection** occurs because some animals are more likely to find mates than other animals. The two main contributors to sexual selection are **competition** of males and **mate selection** by females. An example of male competition is in the mating practices of the redwing blackbird. Some males have huge territories and numerous mates that they defend. Other males have small territories, and some even have no mates. An example of mate selection by females is the mating practices of peacocks. Male peacocks display large, colorful tail feathers to attract females. Females are more likely to choose males with the larger, more colorful displays.

COEVOLUTION

Coevolution describes a rare phenomenon in which two populations with a close ecological relationship undergo reciprocal adaptations simultaneously and evolve together, affecting each other's evolution. General examples of coevolution include predator and prey, or plant and pollinator, and parasites and their hosts. A specific example of coevolution is the yucca moths and the yucca plants. Yucca plants can only be pollinated by the yucca moths. The yucca moths lay their eggs in the yucca flowers, and their larvae grow inside the ovary.

ADAPTIVE RADIATION

Adaptive radiation is an evolutionary process in which a species branches out and adapts and fills numerous unoccupied ecological niches. The adaptations occur relatively quickly, driven by natural selection and resulting in new phenotypes and possibly new species eventually. An example of adaptive radiation is the finches that Darwin studied on the Galápagos Islands. Darwin recorded 13 different varieties of finches, which differed in the size and shape of their beaks. Through the process of natural selection, each type of finch adapted to the specific environment and specifically the food sources of the island to which it belonged. On newly formed islands with many unoccupied ecological niches, the adaptive radiation process occurred quickly due to the lack of competing species and predators.

EVIDENCE SUPPORTING EVOLUTION

MOLECULAR EVIDENCE

Because all organisms are made up of cells, all organisms are alike on a fundamental level. Cells share similar components, which are made up of molecules. Specifically, all cells contain DNA and RNA. This should indicate that all species descended from a **common ancestor**. Humans and chimpanzees share approximately 98% of their genes in common, while humans and bacteria share approximately 7% of their genes in common suggesting that bacteria and humans are not closely related. Biologists have been able to use DNA sequence comparisons of modern organisms to reconstruct the "root" of the tree of life. The fact that RNA can store information, replicate itself, and code for proteins suggests that RNA could have could have evolved first, followed by DNA.

HOMOLOGY

Homology is the similarity of structures of different species based on a similar anatomy in a common evolutionary ancestor. For instance, the forelimbs of humans, dogs, birds, and whales all have the same basic pattern of the bones. Specifically, all of these organisms have a humerus, radius, and ulna. They are all modifications of the same basic evolutionary structure from a common ancestor. Tetrapods resemble the fossils of extinct transitional animal called the *Eusthenopteron*. This would seem to indicate that evolution primarily modifies preexisting structures.

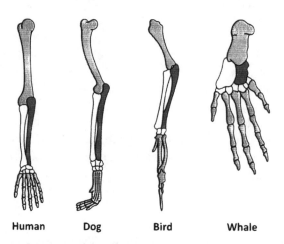

Human   Dog   Bird   Whale

Review Video: <u>Homologous vs Analogous Structures</u>
Visit mometrix.com/academy and enter code: 355157

EMBRYOLOGY

The stages of **embryonic development** reveal homologies between species. These homologies are evidence of a **common ancestor**. For example, in chicken embryos and mammalian embryos, both include a stage in which slits and arches appear in the embryo's neck region that are strikingly similar to gill slits and gill arches in fish embryos. Adult chickens and adult mammals do not have gills, but this embryonic homology indicates that birds and mammals share a common ancestor with fish. As another example, some species of toothless whales have embryos that initially develop teeth that are later absorbed, which indicates that these whales have an ancestor with teeth in the adult form. Finally, most tetrapods have five-digit limbs, but birds have three-digit limbs in their wings. However, embryonic birds initially have five-digit limbs in their wings, which develop into a

three-digit wing. Tetrapods such as reptiles, mammals, and birds all share a common ancestor with five-digit limbs.

ENDOSYMBIOSIS THEORY

The endosymbiosis theory is foundational to evolution. Endosymbiosis provides the path for prokaryotes to give rise to eukaryotes. Specifically, **endosymbiosis** explains the development of the organelles of mitochondria in animals and chloroplasts in plants. This theory states that some eukaryotic organelles such as mitochondria and chloroplasts originated as free living cells. According to this theory, primitive, heterotrophic eukaryotes engulfed smaller, autotrophic bacteria prokaryotes, but the bacteria were not digested. Instead, the eukaryotes and the bacteria formed a symbiotic relationship. Eventually, the bacteria transformed into mitochondrion or chloroplasts.

SUPPORTING EVIDENCE

Several facts support the endosymbiosis theory. Mitochondria and chloroplasts contain their own DNA and can both only arise from other preexisting mitochondria and chloroplasts. The genomes of mitochondria and chloroplasts consist of single, circular DNA molecules with no histones. This is similar to bacteria genomes, not eukaryote genomes. Also, the RNA, ribosomes, and protein synthesis of mitochondria and chloroplasts are remarkably similar to those of bacteria, and both use oxygen to produce ATP. These organelles have a double phospholipid layer that is typical of engulfed bacteria. This theory also involves a secondary endosymbiosis in which the original eukaryotic cells that have engulfed the bacteria are then engulfed themselves by another free-living eukaryote.

CONVERGENT EVOLUTION

Convergent evolution is the evolutionary process in which two or more unrelated species become increasingly similar in appearance. In convergent evolution, similar adaptations in these unrelated species occur due to these species inhabiting the same kind of environment. For example, the mammals shown below, although found in different parts of the world, developed similar appearances due to their similar environments.

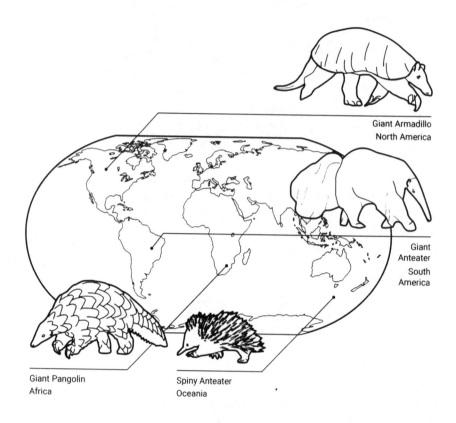

DIVERGENT EVOLUTION

Divergent evolution is the evolutionary process in which organisms of one species become increasingly dissimilar in appearance. As several small adaptations occur due to natural selection, the organisms will finally reach a point at which two new species are formed, also known as **speciation**. Then, these two species will further diverge from each other as they continue to evolve.

Adaptive radiation is an example of divergent evolution. Another example is the divergent evolution of the wooly mammoth and the modern elephant from a common ancestor.

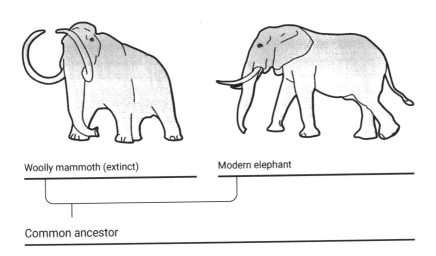

Woolly mammoth (extinct)   Modern elephant

Common ancestor

FOSSIL RECORD

The **fossil record** provides many types of support for evolution including comparisons from rock layers, transition fossils, and homologies with modern organisms. First, fossils from rock layers from all over the world have been compared, enabling scientists to develop a sequence of life from simple to complex. Based on the fossil record, the **geologic timeline** chronicles the history of all living things. For example, the fossil record clearly indicates that invertebrates developed before vertebrates and that fish developed before amphibians. Second, numerous transitional fossils have been found. **Transitional fossils** show an intermediate state between an ancestral form of an organism and the form of its descendants. These fossils show the path of evolutionary change. For example, many transition fossils documenting the evolutionary change from fish to amphibians have been discovered. In 2004, scientists discovered *Tiktaalik roseae*, or the "fishapod," which is a 375-million-year-old fossil that exhibits both fish and amphibian characteristics. Another example would be *Pakicetus*, an extinct land mammal, that scientists determined is an early ancestor of modern whales and dolphins based on the specialized structures of the inner ear. Most fossils exhibit homologies with modern organisms. For example, extinct horses are similar to modern horses, indicating a common ancestor.

CEPHALIZATION AND MULTICELLULARITY

Cephalization is the evolutionary trend that can be summarized as "the evolution of the head." In most animals, nerve tissue has been concentrated into a brain at one end of an organism over many generations. Eventually, a head enclosing a brain and housing sensory organs was produced at one end of the organism. Many invertebrates, such as arthropods and annelids and all vertebrates, have undergone cephalization. However, some invertebrates, such as echinoderms and sponges, have not undergone cephalization, and these organisms literally do not have a head.

Another evolutionary trend is **multicellularity**. Life has evolved from simple, single-celled organisms to complex, multicellular organisms. Over millions of years, single-celled organisms gave rise to biofilms, which gave rise to multicellular organisms, which gave rise to all of the major phyla of multicellular organisms present today.

EXPLANATIONS FOR THE ORIGIN OF LIFE ON EARTH
PANSPERMIA

The word *panspermia* is a Greek work that means "seeds everywhere." **Panspermia** is one possible explanation for the origin of life on Earth that states that "seeds" of life exist throughout the universe and can be transferred from one location to another. Three types of panspermia based on the seed-dispersal method have been proposed. **Lithopanspermia** is described as rocks or dust transferring microorganisms between solar systems. **Ballistic panspermia** is described as rocks or dust transferring microorganisms between planets within the same solar system. **Directed panspermia** is described as intelligent extraterrestrials purposely spreading the seeds to other planets and solar systems. The panspermia hypothesis only proposes the origin of life on Earth. It does not offer an explanation for the origin of life in the universe or explain the origin of the seeds themselves.

ABIOTIC SYNTHESIS OF ORGANIC COMPOUNDS

Scientists have performed sophisticated experiments to determine how the first organic compounds appeared on Earth. First, scientists performed controlled experiments that closely resembled the conditions similar to an early Earth. In the classic **Miller–Urey experiment** (1953), the Earth's early atmosphere was simulated with water, methane, ammonia, and hydrogen that were stimulated by an electric discharge. The Miller–Urey experiment produced complex organic compounds including several amino acids, sugars, and hydrocarbons. Later experiments by other scientists produced nucleic acids. Recently, Jeffrey Bada, a former student of Miller, was able to produce amino acids in a simulation using the Earth's current atmospheric conditions with the addition of iron and carbonate to the simulation. This is significant because in previous studies using Earth's current atmosphere, the amino acids were destroyed by the nitrites produced by the nitrogen.

ATMOSPHERIC COMPOSITION

The early atmosphere of Earth had little or possibly no oxygen. Early rocks had high levels of iron at their surfaces. Without oxygen, the iron just entered into the early oceans as ions. In the same time frame, early photosynthetic algae were beginning to grow abundantly in the early ocean. During photosynthesis, the algae would produce oxygen gas, which oxidized the iron at the rocks' surfaces, forming an iron oxide. This process basically kept the algae in an oxygen-free environment. As the algae population grew much larger, it eventually produced such a large amount of oxygen that it could not be removed by the iron in the rocks. Because the algae at this time were intolerant to oxygen, the algae became extinct. Over time, a new iron-rich layer of sediments formed, and algae populations reformed, and the cycle began again. This cycle repeated itself for millions of years. Iron-rich layers of sediment alternated with iron-poor layers. Gradually, algae and other life forms evolved that were tolerant to oxygen, stabilizing the oxygen concentration in the atmosphere at levels similar to those of today.

DEVELOPMENT OF SELF-REPLICATION

Several hypotheses for the origin of life involve the self-replication of molecules. In order for life to have originated on Earth, proteins and RNA must have been replicated. Hypotheses that combine the replication of proteins and RNA seem promising. One such hypothesis is called **RNA world**. RNA world explains how the pathway of DNA to RNA to protein may have originated by proposing the reverse process. RNA world proposes that self-replicating RNA was the precursor to DNA. Scientists have shown that RNA can actually function both as a gene and as an enzyme and could therefore have carried genetic information in earlier life stages. Also, RNA can be transcribed into DNA using reverse transcription. In RNA world, RNA molecules self-replicated and evolved through recombination and mutations. RNA molecules developed the ability to act as enzymes. Eventually, RNA began to synthesize proteins. Finally, DNA molecules were copied from the RNA in a process of reverse transcription.

HISTORICAL AND CURRENT KINGDOM SYSTEMS

In 1735 Carolus Linnaeus devised a two-kingdom classification system. He placed all living things into either the *Animalia* kingdom or the *Plantae* kingdom. Fungi and algae were classified as plants. Also, Linnaeus developed the binomial nomenclature system that is still used today. In 1866, Ernst Haeckel introduced a three-kingdom classification system, adding the *Protista* kingdom to Linnaeus's animal and plant kingdoms. Bacteria were classified as protists and cyanobacteria were still classified as plants. In 1938, Herbert Copeland introduced a four-kingdom classification system in which bacteria and cyanobacteria were moved to the *Monera* kingdom. In 1969, Robert Whittaker introduced a five-kingdom system that moved fungi from the plant kingdom to the *Fungi* kingdom. Some algae were still classified as plants. In 1977, Carl Woese introduced a six-kingdom system in which in the *Monera* kingdom was replaced with the *Eubacteria* kingdom and the *Archaebacteria* kingdom.

DOMAIN CLASSIFICATION SYSTEM

In 1990, Carl Woese introduced his domain classification system. **Domains** are broader groupings above the kingdom level. This system consists of three domains- *Archaea*, *Bacteria*, and *Eukarya*. All eukaryotes such as plants, animals, fungi, and protists are classified in the *Eukarya* domain. The *Bacteria* and *Archaea* domains consist of prokaryotes. Organisms previously classified in the *Monera* kingdom are now classified into either the *Bacteria* or *Archaea* domain based on their ribosomal RNA structure. Members of the *Archaea* domain often live in extremely harsh environments.

> **Review Video: Biological Classification Systems**
> Visit mometrix.com/academy and enter code: 736052

VIRUSES

Viruses are nonliving, infectious particles that act as parasites in living organisms. Viruses are acellular, which means that they lack cell structure. Viruses cannot reproduce outside of living cells. The structure of a virus is a nucleic acid genome, which may be either DNA or RNA, surrounded by a protective protein coat or **capsid**. In some viruses, the capsid may be surrounded by a lipid membrane or envelope. Viruses can contain up to 500 genes and have various shapes. They usually are too small to be seen without the aid of an electron microscope. Viruses can infect plants, animals, fungi, protists, and bacteria. Viruses can attack only specific types of cells that have specific receptors on their surfaces. Viruses do not divide or reproduce like living cells. Instead, they use the host cell they infect by "reprogramming" it, using the nucleic acid genome, to make more copies of the virus. The host cell usually bursts to release these copies.

> **Review Video: Viruses**
> Visit mometrix.com/academy and enter code: 984455

BACTERIA

Bacteria are small, prokaryotic, single-celled organisms. Bacteria have a circular loop of DNA (plasmid) that is not contained within a nuclear membrane. Bacterial ribosomes are not bound to the endoplasmic reticulum, as in eukaryotes. A cell wall containing peptidoglycan surrounds the bacterial plasma membrane. Some bacteria such as pathogens are further encased in a gel-like, sticky layer called the **capsule**, which enhances their ability to cause disease. Bacteria can be autotrophs or heterotrophs. Some bacterial heterotrophs are saprophytes that function as decomposers in ecosystems. Many types of bacteria share commensal or mutualistic relationships with other organisms. Most bacteria reproduce asexually by binary fission. Two identical daughter cells are produced from one parent cell. Some bacteria can transfer genetic material to other bacteria through a process called conjugation, while some bacteria can incorporate DNA from the environment in a process called transformation.

PROTISTS

Protists are small, eukaryotic, single-celled organisms. Although protists are small, they are much larger than prokaryotic bacteria. Protists have three general forms, which include plantlike protists, animal-like protists, and fungus-like protists. **Plantlike protists** are algae that contain chlorophyll and perform photosynthesis. Animal-like protists are **protozoa** with no cell walls that typically lack chlorophyll and are grouped by their method of locomotion, which may use flagella, cilia, or a different structure. **Fungus-like protists**, which do not have chitin in their cell walls, are generally grouped as either slime molds or water molds. Protists may be autotrophic or heterotrophic. Autotrophic protists include many species of algae, while heterotrophic protists include parasitic, commensal, and mutualistic protozoa. Slime molds are heterotrophic fungus-like protists, which consume microorganisms. Some protists reproduce sexually, but most reproduce asexually by binary fission. Some reproduce asexually by spores while others reproduce by alternation of generations and require two hosts in their life cycle.

FUNGI

Fungi are nonmotile organisms with eukaryotic cells and contain chitin in their cell walls. Most fungi are multicellular, but a few including yeast are unicellular. Fungi have multicellular filaments called **hyphae** that are grouped together into the mycelium. Fungi do not perform photosynthesis and are considered heterotrophs. Fungi can be parasitic, mutualistic or free living. Free-living fungi include mushrooms and toadstools. Parasitic fungi include fungi responsible for ringworm and athlete's foot. Mycorrhizae are mutualistic fungi that live in or near plant roots increasing the roots' surface area of absorption. Almost all fungi reproduce asexually by spores, but most fungi also have a sexual phase in the production of spores. Some fungi reproduce by budding or fragmentation.

> **Review Video: <u>Feeding Among Heterotrophs</u>**
> Visit mometrix.com/academy and enter code: 836017
>
> **Review Video: <u>Kingdom Fungi</u>**
> Visit mometrix.com/academy and enter code: 315081

PLANTS

Plants are multicellular organisms with eukaryotic cells containing cellulose in their cell walls. Plant cells have chlorophyll and perform photosynthesis. Plants can be vascular or nonvascular. **Vascular plants** have true leaves, stems, and roots that contain xylem and phloem. **Nonvascular plants** lack true leaves, stems and roots and do not have any true vascular tissue but instead rely on diffusion and osmosis to transport most of materials or resources needed to survive. Almost all plants are autotrophic, relying on photosynthesis for food. A small number do not have chlorophyll and are parasitic, but these are extremely rare. Plants can reproduce sexually or asexually. Many plants reproduce by seeds produced in the fruits of the plants, while some plants reproduce by seeds on cones. One type of plant, ferns, reproduce by a different system that utilizes spores. Some plants can even reproduce asexually by vegetative reproduction.

STRUCTURE, ORGANIZATION, MODES OF NUTRITION, AND REPRODUCTION OF ANIMALS

Animals are multicellular organism with eukaryotic cells that do not have cell walls surrounding their plasma membranes. Animals have several possible structural body forms. Animals can be relatively simple in structure such as sponges, which do not have a nervous system. Other animals are more complex with cells organized into tissues, and tissues organized into organs, and organs even further organized into systems. Invertebrates such as arthropods, nematodes, and annelids have complex body systems. Vertebrates including fish, amphibians, reptiles, birds, and mammals are the most complex with detailed systems such as those with gills, air sacs, or lungs designed to exchange respiratory gases. All animals are heterotrophs and obtain their nutrition by consuming autotrophs or other heterotrophs. Most animals are motile, but some animals move their environment to bring food to them. All animals reproduce sexually at some point in their life cycle. Typically, this involves the union of a sperm and egg to produce a zygote.

CHARACTERISTICS OF THE MAJOR ANIMAL PHYLA

BODY PLANES

Animals can exhibit bilateral symmetry, radial symmetry, or asymmetry. With **bilateral symmetry**, the organism can be cut in half along only one plane to produce two identical halves. Most animals, including all vertebrates such as mammals, birds, reptiles, amphibians, and fish, exhibit bilateral symmetry. Many invertebrates including arthropods and crustaceans also exhibit bilateral symmetry. With **radial symmetry**, the organism can be cut in half along several planes to produce two identical halves. Starfish, sea urchins, and jellyfish exhibit radial symmetry. With **asymmetry**, the organism exhibits no symmetry. Very few organisms in the animal phyla exhibit asymmetry, but a few species of sponges are asymmetrical.

BODY CAVITIES

Animals can be grouped based on their types of body cavities. A **coelom** is a fluid-filled body cavity between the alimentary canal and the body wall. The three body plans based on the formation of the coelom are coelomates, pseudocoelomates, and acoelomates. **Coelomates** have a true coelom located within the mesoderm. Most animals including arthropods, mollusks, annelids, echinoderms, and chordates are coelomates. **Pseudocoelomates** have a body cavity called a pseudocoelom. **Pseudocoeloms** are not considered true coeloms. Pseudocoeloms are located between mesoderm and endoderm instead of actually in the mesoderm as in a true coelom. Pseudocoelomates include roundworms and rotifers. **Acoelomates** do not have body cavities. Simple or primitive animals such as sponges, jellyfish, sea anemones, hydras, flatworms, and ribbon worms are acoelomates.

MODES OF REPRODUCTION

Animals can reproduce sexually or asexually. Most animals reproduce sexually. In **sexual reproduction**, males and females have different reproductive organs that produce **gametes**. Males have testes that produce sperm, and females have ovaries that produce eggs. During fertilization, a sperm cell unites with an egg cell, forming a **zygote**. Fertilization can occur internally such as in most mammals and birds or externally such as aquatic animals such as fish and frogs. The zygote undergoes cell division, which develops into an embryo and eventually develops into an adult organism. Some embryos develop in eggs such as in fish, amphibians, reptiles, and birds. Some mammals are **oviparous** meaning that they lay eggs, but most are **viviparous** meaning they have a uterus in which the embryo develops. One particular type of mammal called **marsupials** give birth to an immature fetus that finishes development in a pouch. However, there are some animals reproduce **asexually**. For example, hydras reproduce by budding, and starfish and planarians can reproduce by fragmentation and regeneration. Some fish, frogs, and insects can even reproduce by parthenogenesis, which is a type of self-reproduction without fertilization.

MODES OF TEMPERATURE REGULATION

Animals can be classified as either homeotherms or poikilotherms. **Homeotherms**, also called warm-blooded animals or **endotherms**, maintain a constant body temperature regardless of the temperature of the environment. Homeotherms such as mammals and birds have a high metabolic rate because a lot of energy is needed to maintain the constant temperature. **Poikilotherms**, also called cold-blooded animals or **ectotherms**, do not maintain a constant body temperature. Their body temperature fluctuates with the temperature of the environment. Poikilotherms such as arthropods, fish, amphibians, and reptiles have metabolic rates that fluctuate with their body temperature.

ORGANIZATIONAL HIERARCHY WITHIN MULTICELLULAR ORGANISMS

Cells are the smallest living units of organisms. Tissues are groups of cells that work together to perform a specific function. Organs are groups of tissues that work together to perform a specific function. Organ systems are groups of organs that work together to perform a specific function. An organism is an individual that contains several body systems.

CELLS

Cells are the basic structural units of all living things. Cells are composed of various molecules including proteins, carbohydrates, lipids, and nucleic acids. All animal cells are eukaryotic and have a nucleus, cytoplasm, and a cell membrane. Organelles include mitochondria, ribosomes, endoplasmic reticulum, Golgi apparatuses, and vacuoles. Specialized cells are numerous, including but not limited to, various muscle cells, nerve cells, epithelial cells, bone cells, blood cells, and cartilage cells. Cells are grouped to together in tissues to perform specific functions.

TISSUES

Tissues are groups of cells that work together to perform a specific function. Tissues can be grouped into four broad categories: muscle tissue, connective tissue, nerve tissue, and epithelial tissue. Muscle tissue is involved in body movement. **Muscle tissues** can be composed of skeletal muscle cells, cardiac muscle cells, or smooth muscle cells. Skeletal muscles include the muscles commonly called biceps, triceps, hamstrings, and quadriceps. Cardiac muscle tissue is found only in the heart. Smooth muscle tissue provides tension in the blood vessels, controls pupil dilation, and aids in peristalsis. **Connective tissues** include bone tissue, cartilage, tendons, ligaments, fat, blood, and lymph. **Nerve tissue** is located in the brain, spinal cord, and nerves. **Epithelial tissue** makes up the layers of the skin and various membranes. Tissues are grouped together as organs to perform specific functions.

ORGANS AND ORGAN SYSTEMS

Organs are groups of tissues that work together to perform specific functions. **Organ systems** are groups of organs that work together to perform specific functions. Complex animals have several organs that are grouped together in multiple systems. In mammals, there are 11 major organ systems: integumentary system, respiratory system, cardiovascular system, endocrine system, nervous system, immune system, digestive system, excretory system, muscular system, skeletal system, and reproductive system.

MAINTENANCE OF HOMEOSTASIS IN ORGANISMS

ROLE OF FEEDBACK MECHANISMS

Homeostasis is the regulation of internal chemistry to maintain a constant internal environment. This state is controlled through various feedback mechanisms that consist of receptors, an integrator, and effectors. **Receptors** such as mechanoreceptors or thermoreceptors in the skin detect the stimuli. The **integrator** such as the brain or spinal cord receives the information concerning the stimuli and sends out signals to other parts of the body. The **effectors** such as muscles or glands respond to the stimulus. Basically, the receptors receive the stimuli and notify the integrator, which signals the effectors to respond.

Feedback mechanisms can be negative or positive. **Negative-feedback** mechanisms are mechanisms that provide a decrease in response with an increase in stimulus that inhibits the stimulus, which in turn decreases the response. **Positive-feedback** mechanisms are mechanisms that provide an increase in response with an increase in stimulus, which actually increases the stimulus, which in turn increases the response.

ROLE OF HYPOTHALAMUS

The hypothalamus plays a major role in the homoeostasis of vertebrates. The **hypothalamus** is the central portion of the brain just above the brainstem and is linked to the endocrine system through the pituitary gland. The hypothalamus releases special hormones that influence the secretion of pituitary hormones. The hypothalamus regulates the fundamental physiological state by controlling body temperature, hunger, thirst, sleep, behaviors related to attachment, sexual development, fight-or-flight stress response, and circadian rhythms.

ROLE OF ENDOCRINE SYSTEM AND HORMONES

All vertebrates have an **endocrine system** that consists of numerous ductless glands that produce hormones to help coordinate many functions of the body. **Hormones** are signaling molecules that are received by receptors. Many hormones are secreted in response to signals from the pituitary gland and hypothalamus gland. Other hormones are secreted in response to signals from inside the body. Hormones can consist of amino acids, proteins, or lipid molecules such as steroid hormones. Hormones can affect target cells, which have the correct receptor that is able to bind to that particular hormone. Most cells have receptors for more than one type of hormone. Hormones are distributed to the target cells in the blood by the cardiovascular system. Hormones incorporate feedback mechanisms to help the body maintain homeostasis.

ROLE OF ANTIDIURETIC HORMONE

Antidiuretic hormone (ADH) helps maintain homeostasis in vertebrates. ADH is produced by the posterior pituitary gland, and it regulates the reabsorption of water in the kidneys and concentrates the urine. The stimulus in this feedback mechanism is a drop in blood volume due to water loss. This signal is picked up by the hypothalamus, which signals the pituitary gland to secrete ADH. ADH is carried by the cardiovascular system to the nephrons in the kidneys signaling them to reabsorb more water and send less out as waste. As more water is reabsorbed, the blood volume increases, which is monitored by the hypothalamus. As the blood volume reaches the set point, the hypothalamus signals for a decrease in the secretion of ADH, and the cycle continues.

ROLE OF INSULIN AND GLUCAGON

Insulin and glucagon are hormones that help maintain the glucose concentration in the blood. Insulin and glucagon are secreted by the clumps of endocrine cells called the **pancreatic islets** that are located in the pancreas. Insulin and glucagon work together to maintain the blood glucose level. **Insulin** stimulates cells to remove glucose from the blood. **Glucagon** stimulates the liver to convert glycogen to glucose. After eating, glucose levels increase in the blood. This stimulus signals the pancreas to stop the secretion of glucagon and to start secreting insulin. Cells respond to the insulin and remove glucose from the blood, lowering the level of glucose in the blood. Later, after eating, the level of glucose in the blood decreases further. This stimulus signals the pancreas to secrete glucagon and decrease the secretion of insulin. In response to the stimulus, the liver converts glycogen to glucose, and the level of glucose in the blood rises. When the individual eats, the cycle begins again.

THERMOREGULATION

Animals exhibit many adaptations that help them achieve homeostasis, or a stable internal environment. Some of these adaptions are behavioral. Most organisms exhibit some type of behavioral **thermoregulation**. Thermoregulation is the ability to keep the body temperature within certain boundaries. The type of behavioral thermoregulation depends on whether the animal is an endotherm or an ectotherm. **Ectotherms** are "cold-blooded," and their body temperature changes with their external environment. To regulate their temperature, ectotherms often move to an appropriate location. For example, fish move to warmer waters while animals will climb to higher grounds. **Diurnal ectotherms** such as reptiles often bask in the sun to increase their body temperatures. Butterflies are **heliotherms** in that they derive nearly all of their heat from basking in the sun. **Endotherms** are "warm-blooded" and maintain a stable body temperature by internal means. However, many animals that live in hot environments have adapted to the nocturnal lifestyle. Desert animals are often nocturnal to escape high daytime temperatures. Other nocturnal animals sleep during the day in underground burrows or dens.

GAMETE FORMATION

Gametogenesis is the formation of gametes, or reproductive cells. Gametes are produced by meiosis. **Meiosis** is a special type of cell division that consists of two consecutive mitotic divisions referred to as meiosis I and meiosis II. **Meiosis I** is a reduction division in which a diploid cell is reduced to two haploid daughter cells that contain only one of each pair of homologous chromosomes. During **meiosis II**, those haploid cells are further divided to form four haploid cells. **Spermatogenesis** in males produces four viable sperm cells from each complete cycle of meiosis. **Oogenesis** produces four daughter cells, but only one is a viable egg and the other three are polar bodies.

FERTILIZATION

Fertilization is the union of a sperm cell and an egg cell to produce a zygote. Many sperm may bind to an egg, but only one joins with the egg and injects its nuclei into the egg. Fertilization can be external or internal. **External fertilization** takes place outside of the female's body. For example, many fish, amphibians, crustaceans, mollusks, and corals reproduce externally by **spawning** or releasing gametes into the water simultaneously or right after each other. Reptiles and birds reproduce by **internal fertilization**. All mammals except monotremes (e.g. platypus) reproduce by internal fertilization.

EMBRYONIC DEVELOPMENT

Embryonic development in animals is typically divided into four stages: cleavage, patterning, differentiation, and growth. **Cleavage** occurs immediately after fertilization when the large single-celled zygote immediately begins to divide into smaller and smaller cells without an increase in mass. A hollow ball of cells forms a blastula. Next, during patterning, gastrulation occurs. During gastrulation, the cells are organized into three primary germ layers: ectoderm, mesoderm, and endoderm. Then, the cells in these layers differentiate into special tissues and organs. For example, the nervous system develops from the ectoderm. The muscular system develops from the mesoderm. Much of the digestive system develops from the endoderm. The final stage of embryonic development is growth and further tissue specialization. The embryo continues to grow until ready for hatching or birth.

POSTNATAL GROWTH

Postnatal growth occurs from hatching or birth until death. The length of the postnatal growth depends on the species. Elephants can live 70 years, but mice only about 4 years. Right after animals are hatched or born, they go through a period of rapid growth and development. In vertebrates, bones lengthen, muscles grow in bulk, and fat is deposited. At maturity, bones stop growing in length, but bones can grow in width and repair themselves throughout the animal's lifetime, and muscle deposition slows down. Fat cells continue to increase and decrease in size throughout the animal's life. Growth is controlled by genetics but is also influenced by nutrition and disease. Most animals are sexually mature in less than two years and can produce offspring.

VASCULAR AND NONVASCULAR PLANTS

Vascular plants, also referred to as **tracheophytes**, have dermal tissue, meristematic tissue, ground tissues, and vascular tissues. Nonvascular plants, also referred to as **bryophytes**, do not have the vascular tissue xylem and phloem. Vascular plants can grow very tall, whereas nonvascular plants are short and close to the ground. Vascular plants can be found in dry regions, but nonvascular plants typically grow near or in moist areas. Vascular plants have leaves, roots, and stems, but nonvascular plants have leaf-like, root-like, and stem-like structures that do not have true vascular tissue. Nonvascular plants have hair-like **rhizoids**, that act like roots by anchoring them to the ground and absorbing water. Vascular plants include angiosperms, gymnosperms, and ferns. Nonvascular plants include mosses and liverworts.

FLOWERING VERSUS NONFLOWERING PLANTS

Angiosperms and gymnosperms are both vascular plants. **Angiosperms** are flowering plants, and **gymnosperms** are non-flowering plants. Angiosperms reproduce by seeds that are enclosed in an ovary, usually in a fruit, while gymnosperms reproduce by unenclosed or "naked" seeds on scales, leaves, or cones. Angiosperms can be further classified as either monocots or dicots, depending on if they have one or two cotyledons, respectively. Angiosperms include grasses, garden flowers, vegetables, and broadleaf trees such as maples, birches, elms, and oaks. Gymnosperms include conifers such as pines, spruces, cedars, and redwoods.

> **Review Video: Fruits in Flowering Plants**
> Visit mometrix.com/academy and enter code: 867090
>
> **Review Video: Kingdom Plantae Characteristics**
> Visit mometrix.com/academy and enter code: 710084

MONOCOTS AND DICOTS

Angiosperms can be classified as either monocots or dicots. The seeds of **monocots** have one cotyledon, and the seeds of **dicots** have two cotyledons. The flowers of monocots have petals in multiples of three, and the flowers of dicots have petals in multiples of four or five. The leaves of monocots are slender with parallel veins, while the leaves of dicots are broad and flat with branching veins. The vascular bundles in monocots are distributed throughout the stem, whereas the vascular bundles in dicots are arranged in rings. Monocots have a **fibrous root system**, and dicots have a **taproot system**.

PLANT DERMAL TISSUE

Plant dermal tissue is called the epidermis, and is usually a single layer of closely-packed cells that covers leaves and young stems. The epidermis protects the plant by secreting the cuticle, which is a waxy substance that helps prevent water loss and infections. The epidermis in leaves has tiny pores called **stomata**. Guard cells in the epidermis control the opening and closing of the stomata. The epidermis usually does not have chloroplasts. The epidermis may be replaced by periderm in older plants. The **periderm** is also referred to as bark. The layers of the periderm are cork cells or phellem, phelloderm, and cork cambium or phellogen. Cork is the outer layer of the periderm and consists of nonliving cells. The periderm protects the plant and provides insulation.

PLANT VASCULAR TISSUE

The two major types of plant vascular tissue are xylem and phloem. Xylem and phloem are bound together in vascular bundles. A meristem called vascular cambium is located between the xylem and phloem and produces new xylem and phloem. **Xylem** is made up of tracheids and vessel elements. All vascular plants contain tracheids, but only angiosperms contain vessel elements. Xylem provides support and transports water and dissolved minerals unidirectionally from the roots upward using processes like transpiration pull and root pressure. Phloem is made up of companion cells and sieve-tube cells. **Phloem** transports dissolved sugars produced during photosynthesis and other nutrients bidirectionally to non-photosynthetic areas of the plant. By active transport, the companion vessels move glucose in and out of the sieve-tube cells.

PLANT GROUND TISSUE

The three major types of ground tissue are parenchyma tissue, collenchyma tissue, and sclerenchyma tissue. Most ground tissue is made up of parenchyma. **Parenchyma** is formed by parenchyma cells, and it function in photosynthesis, food storage, and tissue repair. The inner tissue of a leaf, mesophyll, is an example of parenchyma tissue. **Collenchyma** is made of collenchyma cells and provides support in roots, stems, and petioles. **Sclerenchyma** tissue is made of sclereid cells, which are more rigid than the collenchyma cells, and provides rigid support and protection. Plant sclerenchyma tissue may contain cellulose or lignin. Fabrics such as jute, hemp, and flax are made of sclerenchyma tissue.

PLANT MERISTEMATIC TISSUE

Meristems or meristematic tissues are regions of plant growth. The cells in meristems are undifferentiated and always remain **totipotent**, which means they can always develop into any type of special tissue. Meristem cells can divide and produce new cells, which can aid in the process of regenerating damaged parts. Cells of meristems reproduce asexually through mitosis or cell division that is regulated by hormones. The two types of meristems are lateral meristems and apical meristems. **Primary growth** occurs at **apical meristems**, located at the tip of roots and shoots, and increases the length of the plant. Primary meristems include the protoderm, which produces epidermis; the procambium, which produces cambium, or lateral meristems; xylem and phloem; and the ground meristem, which produces ground tissue including parenchyma. **Secondary growth** occurs at the lateral or secondary meristems and causes an increase in diameter or thickness.

FLOWERS

The primary function of flowers is to produce seeds for reproduction of the plant. Flowers have a **pedicel**, a stalk with a receptacle or enlarged upper portion, which holds the developing seeds. Flowers also can have sepals and petals. **Sepals** are leaflike structures that protect the bud. **Petals**, which are collectively called the corolla, help to attract pollinators. Plants can have stamens, pistils, or both depending on the type of plant. The **stamen** consists of the anther and filament. The end of the stamen is called the **anther** and is where pollen is produced. Pollen also contains sperm, which is needed in order for a proper plant zygot to form. The **pistil** consists of the stigma, style, and ovary. The ovary contains the ovules, which house the egg cells.

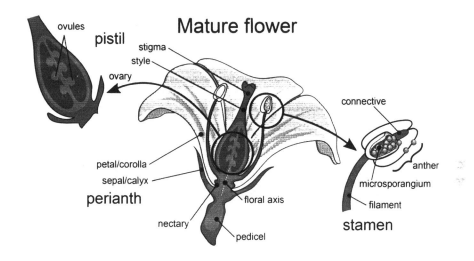

STEMS

Plants can have either woody or nonwoody (herbaceous) stems. **Woody** stems consist of wood, or bark, as a structural tissue, while **herbaceous** stems are very flexible. The stem is divided into nodes and internodes. Buds are located at the nodes and may develop into leaves, roots, flowers, cones, or more stems. Stems consist of dermal tissue, ground tissue, and vascular tissue. **Monocot stems have vascular bundles distributed through the stem. Dicots have rings of vascular bundles**. Stems have four main functions: (1) they provide support to leaves, flowers, and fruits;

(2) they transport materials in the xylem and phloem; (3) they store food; and (4) they have meristems, which provide all of the new cells for the plant.

MONOCOT		DICOT	
Single Cotyledon		Two Cotyledon	
Long Narrow Leaf Parallel Veins		Broad Leaf Network of Veins	
Vascular Bundles Scattered		Vascular Bundles in a Ring	
Floral Parts in Multiples of 3		Floral Parts in Multiples of 4 or 5	

LEAVES

The primary function of a **leaf** is to manufacture food through photosynthesis. The leaf consists of a flat portion called the **blade** and a stalk called the **petiole**. The edge of the leaf is called the margin and can be entire, toothed, or lobed. Veins transport food and water and make up the skeleton of the leaf. The large central vein is called the **midrib**. The blade has an upper and lower epidermis. The epidermis is covered by a protective cuticle. The lower epidermis contains many stomata, which are pores that allow air to enter and leave the leaf. Stomata also regulate transpiration. The middle portion of the leaf is called the **mesophyll**. The mesophyll consists of the palisade mesophyll and the spongy mesophyll. Most photosynthesis occurs in chloroplasts located in the palisade mesophyll.

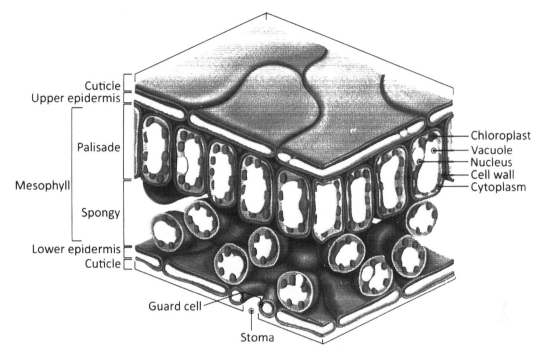

ROOTS

The primary functions of roots are to anchor the plant, absorb materials, and store food. The two basic types of root systems are taproot systems and fibrous root systems. **Taproot systems** have a primary root with many smaller secondary roots. **Fibrous root systems**, which lack a primary root, consist of a mass of many small secondary roots. The root has three main regions: the area of maturation, the area of elongation, and the area of cell division or the meristematic region. The root is covered by an epidermal cell, some of which develops into root hairs. **Root hairs** absorb water and minerals by osmosis, and capillary action helps move the water upward through the roots to the rest of the plant. The center of the root is the **vascular cylinder**, which contains the xylem and phloem. The vascular cylinder is surrounded by the cortex where the food is stored. Primary growth occurs at the root tip. Secondary growth occurs at the vascular cambium located between the xylem and phloem.

POLLINATION STRATEGIES

Pollination is the transfer of pollen from the anther of the stamen to the stigma of the pistil on the same plant or on a different plant. Pollinators can be either **abiotic** (not derived from a living organism) or **biotic** (derived from a living organism). Abiotic pollinators include wind and water. Approximately 20% of pollination occurs by abiotic pollinators. For example, grasses are typically pollinated by wind, and aquatic plants are typically pollinated by water. Biotic pollinators include insects, birds, mammals, and occasionally reptiles. Most biotic pollinators are insects. Many plants have colored petals and strong scents, which attract insects. Pollen rubs off on the insects and is transferred as they move from plant to plant.

SEED DISPERSAL METHODS

Methods of **seed dispersal** can be abiotic or biotic. Methods of seed dispersal include gravity, wind, water, and animals. Some plants produce seeds in fruits that get eaten by animals and then are distributed to new locations in the animals' waste. Some seeds (e.g. dandelions) have structures to aid in dispersal by wind. Some seeds have barbs that get caught in animal hair or bird feathers and are then carried to new locations by the animals. Interestingly, some animals bury seeds for food storage but do not return for the seeds. The seeds of aquatic plants can be dispersed by water, while the seeds of plants near rivers, streams, lakes, and beaches (e.g. coconuts) are also often dispersed by water. Some plants, in a method called **mechanical dispersal**, can propel or shoot their seeds away from them even up to several feet. For example, touch-me-nots and violets utilize mechanical dispersal.

ALTERNATION OF GENERATIONS

Alternation of generations, also referred to as **metagenesis**, contains both a sexual phase and an asexual phase in the life cycle of the plant. Mosses and ferns reproduce by alternation of generations: the sexual phase is called the **gametophyte**, and the asexual phase is called the **sporophyte**. During the sexual phase, a sperm fertilizes an egg to form a zygote. By mitosis, the zygote develops into the sporophyte. The sporangia in the sori of the sporophyte produce the spores through meiosis. The spores germinate and by mitosis produce the gametophyte.

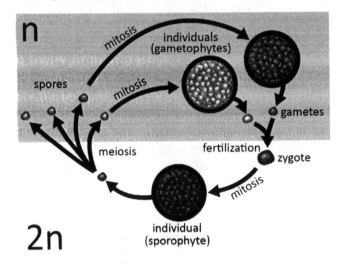

OBTAINING AND TRANSPORTING WATER AND INORGANIC NUTRIENTS

Inorganic nutrients and water enter plants through the root hair and travel to the xylem. Once the water, minerals, and salts have crossed the endodermis, they must be moved upward through the xylem by water uptake. Most of a plant's water is lost through the stomata by transpiration. This loss is necessary to provide the tension needed to pull the water and nutrients up through the xylem. In order to maintain the remaining water that is necessary for the functioning of the plant, guard cells control the stomata. Whether an individual stoma is closed or open is controlled by two guard cells. When the guard cells lose water and become flaccid, they collapse together, closing the stoma. When the guard cells swell with water and become turgid, they move apart, opening the stoma.

USE OF ROOTS

Plant roots have numerous root hairs that absorb water and inorganic nutrients such as minerals and salts. Root hairs are thin, hair-like outgrowths of the root's epidermal cells that exponentially increase the root's surface area. Water molecules cross the cell membranes of the root hairs by **osmosis** and then travel on to the vascular cylinder. Inorganic nutrients are transported across the cell membranes of the root endodermis by **active transport**. The endodermis is a single layer of cells that the water and nutrients must pass through by osmosis or active transport. To control mineral uptake by the roots, Casparian strips act as an extracellular diffusion barrier, and forces nutrients to be pulled into the plant. While water passes through by osmosis, mineral uptake is controlled by transport proteins.

USE OF XYLEM

The xylem contains dead, water-conducting cells called tracheids and vessels. The movement of water upward through the tracheids and vessels is explained by the **cohesion-tension theory**. First, water is lost through evaporation of the plant's surface through transpiration. This can occur at any surface exposed to air but is mainly through the stomata in the epidermis. This transpiration puts the water inside the xylem in a state of tension. Because water is cohesive due to the strong hydrogen bonds between molecules, the water is pulled up the xylem as long as the water is transpiring.

GLUCOSE PRODUCED DURING PHOTOSYNTHESIS

Plants produce glucose, a simple carbohydrate or monosaccharide, during photosynthesis. Plants do not transport glucose molecules directly, but instead glucose undergoes reactions to form sucrose, starch, and cellulose which are then used in different ways. Glucose is joined to a fructose molecule to form **sucrose**, a disaccharide, which is transported in sap. Like glucose, sucrose is also considered a simple carbohydrate. Starches and cellulose are complex carbohydrates consisting of long chains of glucose molecules called polysaccharides. Plants use **starch** to store glucose, and **cellulose** for rigidity in cell walls.

USE OF PHLOEM TO TRANSPORT PRODUCTS OF PHOTOSYNTHESIS

The movement of sugars and other materials from the leaves to other tissues throughout the plants is called **translocation**. Nutrients are translocated from **sources**, or areas with excess sugars such as mature leaves, to **sinks**, areas where sugars are needed (i.e. roots or developing seeds). Phloem vessels are found in the vascular bundles along with the xylem. Phloem contains conducting cells called sieve elements, which are connected end to end in sieve tubes. **Sieve tubes** carry sap from sugar sources to sugar sinks. Phloem sap contains mostly sucrose dissolved in water. The sap can also contain proteins, amino acids, and hormones. Some plants transport sugar alcohols. Loading the sugar into the sieve tubes causes water to enter the tubes by osmosis, creating a higher hydrostatic pressure at the source end of the tube. This pressure is what causes nutrients to move upward towards the sink areas. Sugar is removed from the sieve tube at the sink end and the solute potential is increased, thus causing water to leave the phloem. This process is referred to as the **pressure-flow mechanism**.

Ecology

BIOSPHERE

COMPONENTS

The **biosphere** is the region of the earth inhabited by living things. The components of the biosphere from smallest to largest are organisms, populations, communities, ecosystems, and biomes. Organisms of the same species make up a **population**. All of the populations in an area make up the **community**. The community combined with the physical environment for a region forms an **ecosystem**. Several ecosystems are grouped together to form large geographic regions called **biomes**.

POPULATION

A **population** is a group of all the individuals of one species in a specific area or region at a certain time. A **species** is a group of organisms that can breed and produce fertile offspring. There may be many populations of a specific species in a large geographic region. **Ecologists** study the size, density, and growth rate of populations to determine their stability. Population size continuously changes with births, deaths, and migrations. The population density is the number of individuals per unit of area. Growth rates for a population may be exponential or logistic. Ecologists also study how the individuals are dispersed within a population. Some species form clusters, while others are evenly or randomly spaced. However, every population has limiting factors. Changes in the environment or geography can reduce or limit population size. The individuals of a population interact with each other and with other organisms in the community in various ways, including competition and predation, which have direct impacts population size.

COMMUNITY INTERACTIONS

A **community** is all of the populations of different species that live in an area and interact with each other. Community interaction can be intraspecific or interspecific. **Intraspecific interactions** occur between members of the same species. **Interspecific interactions** occur between members of different species. Different types of interactions include competition, predation, and symbiosis. Communities with high diversity are more complex and more stable than communities with low diversity. The level of diversity can be seen in a food web of the community, which shows all the feeding relationships within the community.

ECOSYSTEMS

An **ecosystem** is the basic unit of ecology. An ecosystem is the sum of all the biotic and abiotic factors in an area. **Biotic factors** are all living things such as plants, animals, fungi, and microorganisms. **Abiotic factors** include the light, water, air, temperature, and soil in an area. Ecosystems obtain the energy they need from sunlight. Ecosystems also contain biogeochemical cycles such as the hydrologic cycle and the nitrogen cycle. Ecosystems are generally classified as either terrestrial or aquatic. All of the living things within an ecosystem are called its community. The number and variety of living things within a community describes the ecosystem's **biodiversity**. However, each ecosystem can only support a limited number of organisms known as the **carrying capacity**.

SYMBIOSIS

Many species share a special nutritional relationship with another species, called **symbiosis**. The term symbiosis means "living together." In symbiosis, two organisms share a close physical relationship that can be helpful, harmful, or neutral for each organism. Three forms of symbiotic relationships are parasitism, commensalism, and mutualism. **Parasitism** is a relationship between two organisms in which one organism is the parasite, and the other organism is the host. The parasite benefits from the relationship because the parasite obtains its nutrition from the host. The host is harmed from the relationship because the parasite is using the host's energy and giving nothing in return. For example, a tick and a dog share a parasitic relationship in which the tick is the parasite, and the dog is the host. **Commensalism** is a relationship between two organisms in which one benefits, and the other is not affected. For example, a small fish called a remora can attach to the belly of a shark and ride along. The remora is safe under the shark, and the shark is not affected. **Mutualism** is a relationship between two organisms in which both organisms benefit. For example, a rhinoceros usually can be seen with a few tick birds perched on its back. The tick birds are helped by the easy food source of ticks, and the rhino benefits from the tick removal.

PREDATION

Predation is a special nutritional relationship in which one organism is the predator, and the other organism is the prey. The predator benefits from the relationship, but the prey is harmed. The predator hunts and kills the prey for food. The predator is specially adapted to hunt its prey, and the prey is specially adapted to escape its predator. While predators harm (kill) their individual prey, predation usually helps the prey species. Predation keeps the population of the prey species under control and prevents them from overshooting the carrying capacity, which often leads to starvation. Also, predation usually helps to remove weak or slow members of the prey species leaving the healthier, stronger, and better adapted individuals to reproduce. Examples of predator-prey relationships include lions and zebras, snakes and rats, and hawks and rabbits.

COMPETITION AND TERRITORIALITY

Competition is a relationship between two organisms in which the organisms compete for the same vital resource that is in short supply. Typically, both organisms are harmed, but one is usually harmed more than the other, which provides an avenue for natural selection. Organisms compete for resources such as food, water, mates, and space. **Interspecific competition** is between members of different species, while **intraspecific competition** is between members of the same species. **Territoriality** can be considered to be a type of interspecific competition for space. Many animals including mammals, birds, reptiles, fish, spiders, and insects have exhibited territorial behavior. Once territories are established, there are fewer conflicts between organisms. For example, a male redwing blackbird can establish a large territory. By singing and flashing his red patches, he is able to warn other males to avoid his territory, and they can avoid fighting.

ALTRUISTIC BEHAVIORS BETWEEN ANIMALS

Altruism is a self-sacrificing behavior in which an individual animal may serve or protect another animal. For example, in a honey bee colony there is one queen with many workers (females). There are also drones (males), but only during the mating seasons. Adult workers do all the work of the hive and will die defending it. Another example of altruism is seen in a naked mole rat colony. Each colony has one queen that mates with a few males, and the rest of the colony is nonbreeding and lives to service the queen, her mates, and her offspring.

> **Review Video: <u>Mutualism, Commensalism, and Parasitism</u>**
> Visit mometrix.com/academy and enter code: 757249

ENERGY FLOW IN THE ENVIRONMENT
USING TROPHIC LEVELS WITH AN ENERGY PYRAMID

Energy flow through an ecosystem can be tracked through an energy pyramid. An **energy pyramid** shows how energy is transferred from one trophic level to another. **Producers** always form the base of an energy pyramid, and the consumers form successive levels above the producers. Producers only store about 1% of the solar energy they receive. Then, each successive level only uses about 10% of the energy of the previous level. That means that **primary consumers** use about 10% of the energy used by primary producers, such as grasses and trees. Next, **secondary**

consumers use 10% of primary consumers' 10%, or 1% overall. This continues up for as many trophic levels as exist in a particular ecosystem.

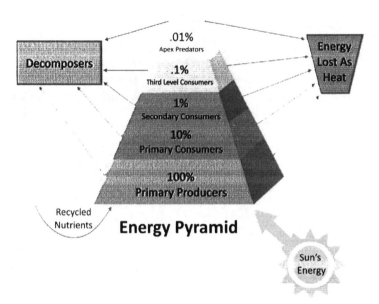

FOOD WEB

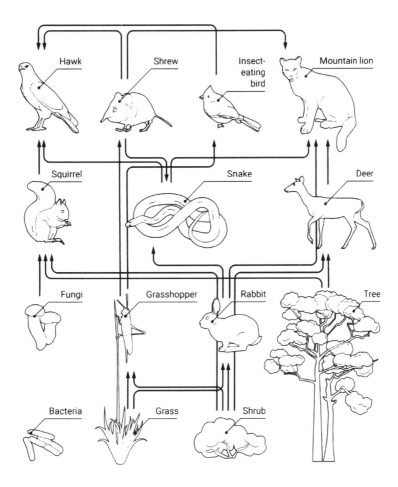

Energy flow through an ecosystem can be illustrated by a **food web**. Energy moves through the food web in the direction of the arrows. In the food web, producers such as grass, trees, and shrubs use energy from the sun to produce food through photosynthesis. Herbivores or primary consumers such as squirrels, grasshoppers, and rabbits obtain energy by eating the producers. Secondary consumers, which are carnivores such as snakes and shrews, obtain energy by eating the primary consumers. Tertiary consumers, which are carnivores such as hawks and mountain lions, obtain energy by eating the secondary consumers. Note that the hawk and the mountain lion can also be considered quaternary consumers in this food web if a different food chain within the web is followed.

> **Review Video: Food Webs**
> Visit mometrix.com/academy and enter code: 853254

Earth Science

PLATE TECTONICS

MAIN CONCEPTS

Plate tectonics is a geological theory that was developed to explain the process of continental drift. The theoretical separation of the Earth's lithosphere and asthenosphere is based upon the

79

mechanical properties of the materials in the two respective layers and is distinct from the chemical separation of Earth's crust, mantle, and core. According to the theory of plate tectonics, the Earth's lithosphere is divided into **ten major plates**: African, Antarctic, Australian, Eurasian, North American, South American, Pacific, Cocos, Nazca, and Indian; it floats atop the asthenosphere. The plates of the lithosphere abut one another at plate boundaries (divergent, convergent, or transform fault), where the formation of topological features of Earth's surface begins.

THEORY

This theory of plate tectonics arose from the fusion of **continental drift** (first proposed in 1915 by Alfred Wegener) and **seafloor spreading** (first observed by Icelandic fishermen in the 1800s and later refined by Harry Hess and Robert Dietz in the early 1960s) in the late 1960s and early 1970s. Prior to this time, the generally accepted explanation for continental drift was that the continents were floating on the Earth's oceans. The discovery that mountains have "roots" (proved by George Airy in the early 1950s) did not categorically disprove the concept of floating continents; scientists were still uncertain as to where those mountainous roots were attached. It was not until the identification and study of the Mid-Atlantic Ridge and magnetic striping in the 1960s that plate tectonics became accepted as a scientific theory. Its conception was a landmark event in the field of Earth sciences—it provided an explanation for the empirical observations of continental drift and seafloor spreading.

TECTONIC PLATE MOTION

The two main sources of **tectonic plate motion** are **gravity** and **friction**. The energy driving tectonic plate motion comes from the dissipation of heat from the mantle in the relatively weak asthenosphere. This energy is converted into gravity or friction to incite the motion of plates. Gravity is subdivided by geologists into ridge-push and slab-pull. In the phenomenon of **ridge-push**, the motion of plates is instigated by the energy that causes low-density material from the mantle to rise at an oceanic ridge. This leads to the situation of certain plates at higher elevations; gravity causes material to slide downhill. In **slab-pull**, plate motion is thought to be caused by cold, heavy plates at oceanic trenches sinking back into the mantle, providing fuel for future convection. Friction is subdivided into mantle drag and trench suction. Mantle drag suggests that plates move due to the friction between the lithosphere and the asthenosphere. Trench suction involves a downward frictional pull on oceanic plates in subduction zones due to convection currents.

> **Review Video: Plate Tectonic Theory**
> Visit mometrix.com/academy and enter code: 535013

CONVERGENT PLATE BOUNDARIES

A **convergent** (destructive) **plate boundary** occurs when adjacent plats move toward one another. The Earth's diameter remains constant over time. Therefore, the formation of new plate material at diverging plate boundaries necessitates the destruction of plate material elsewhere. This process occurs at convergent (destructive) plate boundaries. One plate slips underneath the other at a subduction zone. The results of converging plates vary, depending on the nature of the lithosphere in said plates. When two oceanic plates converge, they form a deep underwater trench. If each of the converging plates at a destructive boundary carries a continent, the light materials of the continental lithosphere enables both plates to float above the subduction area. They crumple and compress, creating a mid-continent mountain range. When a continental plate converges with an oceanic plate, the denser oceanic lithosphere slides beneath the continental lithosphere. The result of such convergence is an oceanic trench on one side and a mountain range on the other.

DIVERGENT PLATE BOUNDARY

A **divergent**, or constructive, **plate boundary** exists when two adjacent plates move away from one another. Observation of activity at diverging boundaries provided unquestionable proof of the seafloor-spreading hypothesis. At this type of plate boundary, kinetic energy generated by asthenospheric convection cells cracks the lithosphere and pushes molten magma through the space left by separating tectonic plates. This magma cools and hardens, creating a new piece of the Earth's crust. In the oceanic lithosphere, diverging plate boundaries form a series of rifts known as the oceanic ridge system. The Mid-Atlantic Ridge is a consequence of undersea diverging boundaries. At divergent boundaries on the continental lithosphere, plate movement results in rift valleys, typified by the East African Rift Valley.

TRANSFORM PLATE BOUNDARY

A **transform** (conservative) **plate boundary** exists when two tectonic plates slide past each other laterally and in opposite directions. Due to the rocky composition of lithospheric plates, this motion causes the plates to grind against each other. Friction causes stress to build when the plates stick; this potential energy is finally released when the built-up pressure exceeds the slipping point of the rocks on the two plates. This sudden release of energy causes earthquakes. This type of plate boundary is also referred to as a **strike-slip fault**. The San Andreas Fault in California is the most famous example of such a boundary.

GEOLOGIC FAULTS

A **geologic fault** is a fracture in the Earth's surface created by movement of the crust. The majority of faults are found along **tectonic plate boundaries**; however, smaller faults have been identified at locations far from these boundaries. There are three types of geologic faults, which are named for the original direction of movement along the active fault line. The landforms on either side of a fault are called the footwall and the hanging wall, respectively. In a **normal fault**, the hanging wall moves downward relative to the footwall. A **reverse fault** is the opposite of a normal fault: The hanging wall moves upward relative to the footwall. The dip of a reverse fault is usually quite steep; when the dip is less than 45 degrees, the fault is called a thrust fault. In the third type of geologic fault, the **strike-slip fault**, the dip is virtually nonexistent, and the footwall moves vertically left (sinistral) or right (dextral). A transform plate boundary is a specific instance of a strike-slip fault.

GEOLOGIC FOLDING

A **geologic fold** is a region of curved or deformed stratified rocks. Folding is one process by which Earth's crust is deformed. Rock strata are normally formed horizontally; however, geologists have identified areas where these strata arc upwards or downwards. **Anticlines** are upfolded areas of rock; downfolds are called synclines. In anticlines, the rocks are oldest along the axis (a horizontal line drawn through the point of the fold's maximum curvature), and in synclines, the youngest rocks are at the axis. **Monoclines**, or flextures, are rock structures that slope in one direction only, and often pass into geologic fault lines. The process of folding usually occurs underneath the Earth's surface, but surface erosion eventually exposes these formations. Folding is generally thought to be caused by the horizontal compression of the Earth's surface, which is related to the movement of tectonic plates and fault activity.

OROGENESIS

Orogenesis refers to mountain-building processes, specifically as they relate to the movement of tectonic plates. An individual orogeny can take millions of years. Generally, mountains are created when compressional forces push surface rock upward, resulting in a landform that is higher than the land around it. There are four broad categories of mountains (which are not mutually exclusive); these categories are based on the mountain's formative origin. **Folded mountains**, formed from the long-term deformation and metamorphosis of sedimentary and igneous rocks, usually occur in chains. This type of mountain often forms at convergent plate boundaries. **Fault-block mountains** occur at normal or reverse faults with high dips. Portions of Earth's crust are vertically displaced along the faults. **Oceanic ridges** are formed at divergent boundaries beneath the ocean. When plates move apart, material from the mantle rises up and creates long mountain chains. **Volcanic mountains** form from the accumulation of products of volcanic eruptions, such as ash and lava. They often occur singularly, unlike other mountain types that usually exist in chains.

CONTINENTAL DRIFT

Continental drift is a theory that explains the separation and movement of the continents based on shifts in a plastic layer of Earth's interior caused by the planet's rotation (seafloor spreading). Continental drift is part of the larger theory of plate tectonics. In the early twentieth century, many scientists and scholars noted that the edges of certain continents seemed to look like connecting pieces of a puzzle. Due to this observation, as well as the fact that similar geologic features, fossils, fauna, and flora existed on the Atlantic coasts of continents like South America and Africa, these observers theorized the previous existence of a supercontinent (referred to as Pangaea), in which all of the discrete continents identifiable today were joined together.

CONTINENTAL CRUST

The **continental crust** (sial) is 10–50 kilometers thick. It is more complex and locally variable than the oceanic crust. There is a correlation between the thickness of the sial and the age of the last orogenic (mountain-forming) event recorded at the surface: The thinnest crust occurs in areas of the oldest orogenic activity, and the thickest crust is located near present-day mountain chains. The continental crust consists of two layers separated by a seismic velocity discontinuity located 8–10 kilometers below the surface. The upper layer has an average density of 2,670 $\frac{kg}{m^3}$ and is composed mainly of granite. This layer exhibits thermal energy related to the activity of radioactive elements. The lower layer has gabbroic properties and an average density of 3,000 $\frac{kg}{m^3}$. The temperature of this layer is thought to be below the melting point of its component rocks and minerals and is extremely variable, depending on the presence of volatiles (elements such as water, carbon dioxide, and sulfur).

OCEANIC CRUST

The **oceanic crust** (sima) is 5–10 kilometers thick. It is remarkably uniform in composition and thickness and consists of a layer of sediments (fossils of marine life and continental debris) that overlies three distinct layers of igneous rock. The first of these is 1–2.5 kilometers thick and is made up of basaltic lavas. The second, main igneous layer is 5 kilometers thick and is of coarse-grained gabbroic composition. The third layer is very thin (less than half a kilometer thick) and possesses a density of 3,000 $\frac{kg}{m^3}$; this layer is made up of basalts. The temperature of the sima is very high along seismically active ridges and lower near oceanic basins. Based on dating of the fossils present in its sediments, scientists estimate that the oceanic crust is only 200 million years old (in comparison, the continental crust is estimated to be several billion years old). The relatively young age of the oceanic crust provides support for theories of the creative/destructive processes of seafloor spreading.

MAGNETIC STRIPING

Magnetic striping is a manifestation of the magnetic properties of the oceanic lithosphere. In general, the mineral composition of rocks has one of two magnetic orientations: normal polarity, which roughly corresponds with the polarity of the Earth's magnetic north, or reversed polarity, which is basically the opposite of the Earth's magnetic field. Cooled magma, which makes up the basalt of the ocean floor, aligns itself with Earth's current magnetic orientation during the cooling process. While the Earth's magnetic field normally shifts very slowly, it undergoes radical changes, called magnetic reversals, over long periods of time. Diverging plate boundaries on the ocean floor have been forming new crust material for tens of thousands of years, creating new midocean ridges throughout multiple reversals of Earth's magnetic field. Consequently, the ocean floor displays stripes of rocks with opposing polarities. The discovery of magnetic striping in the oceanic crust contributed to widespread acceptance of the seafloor-spreading hypothesis.

SEAFLOOR SPREADING

Seafloor spreading was originally put forth as an explanation for the existence of midocean ridges such as the Mid-Atlantic Ridge. These ridges were identified as features of a vast undersea mountain system that spans the globe. Seafloor spreading postulates that the ocean floor expands outward from these ridges. The process occurs when the upper mantle layer of the Earth (the asthenosphere), just beneath the planet's crust, is heated through convection. The heat causes the asthenosphere to become more elastic and less dense. This heated material causes the crust to bow outward and eventually separate. The lighter material then flows out through the resultant rift and hardens, forming new oceanic crust. If a rift opens completely into an ocean, the basin will be flooded with seawater and create a new sea. Often, the process results in failed rifts, rifts that stopped opening before complete separation is achieved.

EARTH'S LAYERS
CHEMICAL LAYERS

The **crust** is the outermost layer of the Earth. It is located 0–35 kilometers below the surface. Earth's crust is composed mainly of basalt and granite. The crust is less dense, cooler, and more rigid than the planet's internal layers. This layer floats on top of the **mantle**. Located 35–2,890 kilometers below the Earth's surface, the mantle is separated from the crust by the **Mohorovicic discontinuity**, or Moho (which occurs at 30–70 kilometers below the continental crust and at 6–8 kilometers beneath the oceanic crust). The mantle is made up of rocks such as peridotite and eclogite; its temperature varies from 100 to 3,500 degrees Celsius. Material in the mantle cycles due to convection. The innermost layer of the Earth is the core, which consists of a liquid outer layer and a solid inner layer. It is located 2,890–6,378 kilometers below the surface. The core is thought to be composed of iron and nickel and is the densest layer of the Earth.

SUBLAYERS

The **lithosphere** consists of the crust and the uppermost portion of the mantle of the Earth. It is located 0–60 kilometers below the surface. The lithosphere is the cooling layer of the planet's convection cycle and thickens over time. This solid shell is fragmented into pieces called tectonic plates. The oceanic lithosphere is made up of mafic basaltic rocks and is thinner and generally more dense than the continental lithosphere (composed of granite and sedimentary rock); the lithosphere floats atop Earth's mantle. The **asthenosphere** is the soft, topmost layer of the mantle. It is located 100–700 kilometers below the surface. A combination of heat and pressure keeps the asthenosphere's composite material plastic. The **mesosphere** is located 900–2,800 kilometers below the surface; it therefore spans from the lower part of the mantle to the mantle-core boundary. The liquid **outer core** exists at 2,890–5,100 kilometers below surface level, and the solid inner core exists at depths of 5,100–6,378 kilometers.

Review Video: Earth's Structure
Visit mometrix.com/academy and enter code: 713016

ROCK CYCLE

The **rock cycle** is the process whereby the materials that make up the Earth transition through the three types of rock: igneous, sedimentary, and metamorphic. Rocks, like all matter, cannot be created or destroyed; rather, they undergo a series of changes and adopt different forms through the functions of the rock cycle. Plate tectonics and the water cycle are the driving forces behind the rock cycle; they force rocks and minerals out of equilibrium and force them to adjust to different external conditions. Viewed in a generalized, cyclical fashion, the rock cycle operates as follows: rocks beneath Earth's surface melt into magma. This **magma** either erupts through volcanoes or remains inside the Earth. Regardless, the magma cools, forming igneous rocks. On the surface, these rocks experience **weathering** and **erosion**, which break them down and distribute the fragments across the surface. These fragments form layers and eventually become **sedimentary rocks**. Sedimentary rocks are then either transformed to **metamorphic rocks** (which will become magma inside the Earth) or melted down into magma.

ROCK FORMATION

Igneous Rocks: Igneous rocks can be formed from sedimentary rocks, metamorphic rocks, or other igneous rocks. Rocks that are pushed under the Earth's surface (usually due to plate subduction) are exposed to high mantle temperatures, which cause the rocks to melt into magma. The magma then rises to the surface through volcanic processes. The lower atmospheric temperature causes the magma to cool, forming grainy, extrusive igneous rocks. The creation of extrusive, or volcanic, rocks is quite rapid. The cooling process can occur so rapidly that crystals do not form; in this case, the result is a glass, such as obsidian. It is also possible for magma to cool down inside the Earth's interior; this type of igneous rock is called intrusive. Intrusive, or plutonic, rocks cool more slowly, resulting in a coarse-grained texture.

Sedimentary Rocks: Sedimentary rocks are formed when rocks at the Earth's surface experience weathering and erosion, which break them down and distribute the fragments across the surface. Fragmented material (small pieces of rock, organic debris, and the chemical products of mineral sublimation) is deposited and accumulates in layers, with top layers burying the materials beneath. The pressure exerted by the topmost layers causes the lower layers to compact, creating solid sedimentary rock in a process called lithification.

Metamorphic Rocks: Metamorphic rocks are igneous or sedimentary rocks that have "morphed" into another kind of rock. In metamorphism, high temperatures and levels of pressure change preexisting rocks physically and/or chemically, which produces different species of rocks. In the rock cycle, this process generally occurs in materials that have been thrust back into the Earth's mantle by plate subduction. Regional metamorphism refers to a large band of metamorphic activity; this often occurs near areas of high orogenic (mountain-building) activity. Contact metamorphism refers to metamorphism that occurs when "country rock" (that is, rock native to an area) comes into contact with high-heat igneous intrusions (magma).

PLATE TECTONICS ROCK CYCLE

The plate tectonics rock cycle expands the concept of the traditional rock cycle to include more specific information about the tectonic processes that propel the rock cycle, as well as an evolutionary component. Earth's materials do not cycle endlessly through the different rock forms; rather, these transitive processes cause, for example, increasing diversification of the rock types found in the crust. Also, the cycling of rock increases the masses of continents by increasing the volume of granite. Thus, the **tectonic rock cycle** is a model of an evolutionary rock cycle. In this model, new oceanic lithosphere is created at divergent plate boundaries. This new crust spreads outward until it reaches a **subduction zone**, where it is pushed back into the mantle, becomes magma, and is thrust out into the **atmosphere**. It experiences erosion and becomes **sedimentary rock**. At convergent continental plate boundaries, this crust is involved in mountain building and the associated metamorphic pressures. It is **eroded** again, and returns to the lithosphere.

ROLE OF WATER

Water plays an important role in the rock cycle through its roles in **erosion** and **weathering**: it wears down rocks; it contributes to the dissolution of rocks and minerals as acidic soil water; and it carries ions and rock fragments (sediments) to basins where they will be compressed into **sedimentary rock**. Water also plays a role in the **metamorphic processes** that occur underwater in newly-formed igneous rock at mid-ocean ridges. The presence of water (and other volatiles) is a vital component in the melting of rocky crust into magma above subduction zones.

> **Review Video: Igneous, Sedimentary, and Metamorphic Rocks**
> Visit mometrix.com/academy and enter code: 689294

METAMORPHISM

Metamorphism is the process whereby existing sedimentary, igneous, or metamorphic rocks (protoliths) are transformed due to a change in their original physiochemical environment, where they were mineralogically stable. This generally happens alongside sedimentation, orogenesis, or the movement of tectonic plates. Between the Earth's surface and a depth of 20 kilometers, there exists a wide range of temperatures, pressure levels, and chemical activity. Metamorphism is generally an **isochemical process**, which means that it does not alter the initial chemical composition of a rock. The changes a rock undergoes in metamorphism are usually physical. Neither a metamorphosing rock nor its component minerals are melted during this process—they remain almost exclusively in a solid state. Metamorphism, like the formation of plutonic rock bodies, can be studied only after metamorphic rocks have been exposed by weathering and erosion of the crustal rocks above.

FACTORS

Heat is a primary factor in metamorphism. When extreme heat is applied to existing rocks, their component minerals are able to recrystallize (which entails a reorganization of the grains or molecules of a mineral, resulting in increased density, as well as the possible expulsion of volatiles such as water and carbon dioxide). High levels of thermal energy may also cause rocks to contort and deform. **Pressure** is another factor affecting the metamorphism of rocks. Increased pressure can initiate recrystallization through compression. Pressure forces can also lead to spot-melting at individual grain boundaries. Lithostatic, or confining, pressure is created by the load of rocks above a metamorphosing rock. Pore-fluid pressure results from the release of volatiles due to thermal energy. Directed pressure is enforced in a certain direction due to orogenesis: This type of pressure is responsible for foliation, or layering, which entails parallel alignment of mineral particles in a rock, characteristic of metamorphism. **Chemical activity** affects metamorphism due to the presence of volatiles in pore fluids.

BIOGEOCHEMICAL CYCLE

The term biogeochemical cycle refers to one of several chemical processes in which chemical elements are (re)cycled among **biotic** (living) and **abiotic** (nonliving) constituents of an ecosystem. The theory of relativity necessitates the presence of such cycles in nature by virtue of its supposition that energy and matter are not created or destroyed in a closed system such as Earth's ecosystem. Generally, a **biogeochemical cycle** operates as follows: inorganic compounds, such as carbon, are converted from water, air, and soil to organic molecules by organisms called **autotrophs**. **Heterotrophs** (organisms that cannot independently produce their own food) consume the autotrophs; some of the newly formed organic molecules are transferred. Finally, the organic molecules are broken down and processed once again into inorganic compounds by secondary and tertiary consumers and replaced within water, air, and soil. Carbon, nitrogen, and phosphorus provide examples of nutrients that are recycled in the Earth's ecosystem.

UNIFORMITARIANISM

Uniformitarianism is a basic tenet of the science disciplines. It states that the processes which made the world the way it is today are still in effect. This means that careful observation and analysis of the natural processes occurring right now can provide information about the processes which formed the world as it is now known. Simply put, it says that "the present is the key to the past."

An associated (but perhaps less generally accepted) idea is that of **gradualism**, which says that the processes which created the world as it is known operated at the same rate that they do now.

The doctrine of **uniformitarianism** is applicable in all scientific disciplines, from geology to the life sciences to astronomy to physics. In geology, uniformitarianism supplanted the theory of catastrophism, which suggested that earth was formed by isolated, catastrophic events, such as a worldwide flood.

STRATIGRAPHIC CORRELATION

The law of **superposition** states that in bodies of undisturbed sedimentary rocks, the strata at the bottom are older than the strata at the top. **Stratigraphic correlation** is a method used to determine the "correct" or natural stratigraphic position of rock beds which have been separated by disturbances such as metamorphic processes, orogenies, or plutonic formations. This is achieved through the identification of correspondence between two points in a characteristic such as fossil content, lithology (the physical characteristics of a rock), or geologic age. This practice of (theoretically) realigning beds which have been deformed is helpful in identification of the relative ages of rocks in a sedimentary rock sequence.

IMPORTANT TERMS

Geological stratum - a layer of rock which possesses certain attributes which distinguishes it from adjacent layers of rock. Such attributes include, but are not limited to, lithology, chemical composition, and mineralogy.

Stratigraphy - the study of the arrangement, form, distribution, composition, and succession of rock strata. Information gained from such study is then used to form hypotheses about the strata's origins, environments, relations to organic environments, relations to other geologic concepts, and ages.

Chronostratigraphy - an aspect of stratigraphy which focuses on the relative ages of geologic strata. Scientists examine the physical interrelations of strata, the relations of strata to the sequence of organic evolution, and radioactive ages of strata to determine their chronological sequence. When the relative ages of strata have been identified, scientists can examine the constituents and properties of those strata for clues about the sequence of events which made the world what it is today.

RECORD OF THE EARTH'S HISTORY
ROCKS

One important way in which rocks provide a record of **earth's history** is through the study of **fossils**, which allows scientists to make inferences about the evolution of life on earth. However, the presentation of fossils is certainly not the only record of earth's history contained in rocks. For instance, the **chemical composition** of rock strata may give indications about the atmospheric and/or hydrospheric compositions at certain points in earth's history. Paleomagnetism constitutes another aspect of earth's historical record contained in rocks. Through the study of magnetic orientations of rocks formed at certain times in history, scientists learn more about the form and function of earth's magnetic field then and now.

SEDIMENTS

The study of the **sediments** which make up sedimentary rocks can reveal much about the environment in which they are formed. For example, a study of the **different types** of sediments in a bed, and the **ratios** in which they occur, can indicate the types of rocks exposed at the origination site and the relative abundances of each. Examination of the sorting of a sediment can reveal information about how far the particles traveled from their provenance, as well as the medium which carried the particles. For example, sediments transported by wind tend to be well-sorted, while water moves large particles which are often worn into spheres. The type of weathering experienced by particles in a sedimentary bed can reveal the climate from which they came—mechanical weathering tends to occur in cold and arid climates, while chemical weathering is more common in hot and humid climates. Interpreting the information supplied by sediment can, in turn, reveal information about past conditions on earth.

SOIL

The study of **soil development** can give indications of the **age of certain sedimentary deposits**. For example, the study of soil led to the idea that multiple glaciations have occurred on the North American continent. Examination of the development level of certain areas of soil can also inform earth scientists about natural catastrophic events which have occurred in the past. Study of soil deposits also aided in the determination of how often "ice ages" can be expected to occur. Also, the presence of certain types of soil buried deep beneath the surface can provide indications of past climates.

PREHISTORIC OCEANS

The elements present in the earliest oceans were quite different from those present in the Earth's hydrosphere today. This is largely due to the chemical composition of the atmosphere at that time. The oceans were formed when cooling caused atmospheric clouds to condense and produce rain. **Volcanic gasses** contributed elements such as sulfur and carbon dioxide to the air. Therefore, scientists suspect that the earliest oceans contained high levels of acids (for example, sulfuric acid, hydrochloric acid, and hydrofluoric acid), and low levels of the salts that inhabit the oceans today. The temperature in this early ocean was probably close to 100 degrees Celsius. As **carbon dioxide** began to dissolve in the water, it combined with carbonate ions to form limestone which was deposited on the ocean floor. Consequently, more carbon dioxide was trapped in these rocks. Eventually, **calcium carbonate** began to reduce the acidity of these early oceans. **Weathering** brought different minerals into the ocean, which began to increase its saltiness toward its current levels.

RADIOMETRIC DATING

Radiometric dating is one of the only methods currently available to determine the absolute age of an object such as a fossil or rock body. This process is possible when such an object contains isotopes, the products of radioactive decay. In radioactive decay, the atoms of certain unstable isotopes are transformed through the emissions of either electrons or alpha particles. This process occurs exponentially until it produces a stable final product. The rate of radioactive decay is measured in half-lives: after one half-life has passed, one-half of the atoms of the original element will have decayed. When scientists examine an object which contains isotopes with known half-life periods, they can determine the amount of the isotope that was present at the time of the object's origin. That figure can then be compared with the present level to determine the age of the object.

GAIA HYPOTHESIS

Named for the Greek goddess who organized a living earth from chaos, the **Gaia hypothesis** states that the planet is a **living system**. While this idea is not scientific in the literal sense, it provides a metaphor which is useful in achieving an understanding of the interconnectedness of all of earth's systems. For example, increased levels of carbon dioxide in the atmosphere breed higher levels of plant growth, and these plants help to regulate the amount of carbon dioxide present in the atmosphere. Feedback mechanisms such as this were known before the formulation of the Gaia hypothesis. However, adherence to this idea requires one to study the planet as a whole, rather than focusing on only one of its many aspects in isolation. The fact that earth's atmosphere is quite different from those of the other planets led to the formulation of this idea.

GEOLOGIC TIME

Geologic time may be measured absolutely using chronometric time, or relatively using chronostratic time. Measurements of chronometric time are achieved through **radiometric dating** and are expressed numerically in number of years. **Chronostratic time**, which places events in sequences, can be estimated through the study of rock bodies. According to the law of original horizontality, the original orientation of sedimentary beds is nearly always horizontal. Therefore, if one observes deformed or slanted strata, the event which disoriented the strata must have occurred after the strata were deposited. Also, a rock body that cuts across another must be newer than the rock body it intersects. Similarly, for a layer of rock to experience erosion and weathering, it must already exist on the surface. These destructive processes can lead to interruptions in the geologic record. Sometimes, sediments are deposited atop a weathered and eroded surface. Such an occurrence is called an unconformity. The most common method used to establish chronostratic time is through stratigraphy, as the name suggests.

Relative geologic time is divided into different units, including two recognized eons: the **Precambrian**, of which little is known due to limited fossil evidence that only reveals ultra-primitive life forms; and the **Phanerozoic**, for which fossil evidence is more abundant and reveals more evolved life forms. **Eons** are the largest units of geologic time.

Scientists also recognize three eras: the Paleozoic, the Mesozoic, and the Cenozoic. Eras contain periods, and periods contain epochs. These units are delineated largely by the conceptions used to divide historical time. They are arranged in a sequence through chronostratigraphy and classified largely on the basis of the fossils found in their associated strata.

PALEONTOLOGY

Paleontology is the study of ancient plant and animal life. The bulk of information on this subject is provided by the fossil record, which consists of fossilized plants, animals, tracks, and chemical residues preserved in rock strata. There are three general subdivisions within the field of paleontology. The first, **paleozoology**, is the study of ancient animal life, including vertebrate and invertebrate specializations, as well as paleoanthropology, the study of fossil hominids. The second is **paleobotany**, the study of ancient plant life. The third, **micropaleontology**, is the study of microfossils. This field of scientific inquiry is useful in identifying the evolutionary processes that gave rise to present-day life forms. Paleontology also contributes to an understanding of the ways that environmental and geological factors affected evolution.

EVOLUTION

Evolution is the process whereby organisms pass certain acquired traits to successive generations, affecting the attributes of later organisms and even leading to the creation of new species. Charles Darwin is the name often associated with the formulation of natural selection, a vital component of evolution as it is known today. **Natural selection** states that members of a species are not identical—due to their respective genetic make-ups, each individual will possess traits which make it stronger or weaker and more or less able to adapt. The other tenet of natural selection is that members of a species will always have to compete for scarce resources to survive. Therefore, organisms with traits which will help them survive are more likely to do so and produce offspring, passing along the "desirable" traits. Darwin suggested that this process, by creating groups of a species with increasingly different characteristics, would eventually lead to the formation of **a new species**.

SIGNIFICANT EVENTS LEADING TO EVOLUTION OF MAN

The **origination of life** is the most fundamental development in the history of life on Earth. Prokaryotic microfossils, the earliest fossils identified by paleontologists, are dated to near 3.5 billion years ago. However, the presence of large amounts of certain carbon and oxygen isotopes in sedimentary rocks dated at about 3.8 billion years ago may indicate the presence of organic material. The next significant event suggested by a drastic change in the fossil record is the huge diversification of species which occurred approximately 543 million years ago, near the end of the Precambrian eon and the beginning of the Phanerozoic. This theoretical evolutionary stage included higher-level tissue organization in multicellular organisms, the development of predator-prey relationships, and, most importantly, the development of skeletons. The final critical step toward the evolution of man is the emergence of life on land about 418 million years ago. This necessitated the evolution of structures which could breathe air, obtain and retain water on land, and support its own weight out of water.

HYDROLOGIC CYCLE

The **hydrologic (water) cycle** refers to the circulation of water in the Earth's hydrosphere (below the surface, on the surface, and above the surface of the Earth). This continuous process involves five physical actions. Evaporation entails the change of water molecules from a liquid to gaseous state. Liquid water on the Earth's surface (often contained in a large body of water) becomes water vapor and enters the atmosphere when its component molecules gain enough kinetic (heat) energy to escape the liquid form. As the vapor rises, it cools and therefore loses its ability to maintain the gaseous form. It begins to the process of condensation (the return to a liquid or solid state) and forms clouds. When the clouds become sufficiently dense, the water falls back to Earth as precipitation. Water is then either trapped in vegetation (interception) or absorbed into the surface (infiltration). Runoff, caused by gravity, physically moves water downward into oceans or other water bodies.

EVAPORATION

Evaporation is the change of state in a substance from a liquid to a gaseous form at a temperature below its boiling point (the temperature at which all of the molecules in a liquid are changed to gas through vaporization). Some of the molecules at the surface of a liquid always maintain enough heat energy to escape the cohesive forces exerted on them by neighboring molecules. At higher temperatures, the molecules in a substance move more rapidly, increasing their number with enough energy to break out of the liquid form. The rate of evaporation is higher when more of the surface area of a liquid is exposed (as in a large water body, such as an ocean). The amount of moisture already in the air also affects the rate of evaporation—if there is a significant amount of water vapor in the air around a liquid, some evaporated molecules will return to the liquid. The speed of the evaporation process is also decreased by increased atmospheric pressure.

CONDENSATION

Condensation is the phase change in a substance from a gaseous to liquid form; it is the opposite of evaporation or vaporization. When temperatures decrease in a gas, such as water vapor, the material's component molecules move more slowly. The decreased motion of the molecules enables intermolecular cohesive forces to pull the molecules closer together and, in water, establish hydrogen bonds. Condensation can also be caused by an increase in the pressure exerted on a gas, which results in a decrease in the substance's volume (it reduces the distance between particles). In the hydrologic cycle, this process is initiated when warm air containing water vapor rises and then cools. This occurs due to convection in the air, meteorological fronts, or lifting over high land formations.

PRECIPITATION

Precipitation is water that falls back to Earth's surface from the atmosphere. This water may be in the form of rain, which is water in the liquid form. Raindrops are formed in clouds due to the process of condensation. When the drops become too heavy to remain in the cloud (due to a decrease in their kinetic energy), gravity causes them to fall down toward Earth's surface. Extremely small raindrops are called drizzle. If the temperature of a layer of air through which rain passes on its way down is below the freezing point, the rain may take the form of sleet (partially frozen water). Precipitation may also fall in the form of snow, or water molecules sublimated into ice crystals. When clumps of snowflakes melt and refreeze, hail is formed. Hail may also be formed when liquid water accumulates on the surface of a snowflake and subsequently freezes.

TRANSPORTATION OF WATER IN THE WATER CYCLE

In the **hydrologic cycle**, the principal movement of water in the atmosphere is its transport from the area above an ocean to an area over land. If this transport did not occur, the hydrologic cycle would be less a cycle than the vertical motion of water from the oceans to the atmosphere and back again. Some evaporated water is transported in the form of clouds consisting of condensed water droplets and small ice crystals. The clouds are moved by the jet stream (strong winds in the upper levels of the atmosphere that are related to surface temperatures) or by surface winds (land or sea breezes). Most of the water that moves through the atmosphere is water vapor (water in the gaseous form).

> **Review Video: Hydrologic Cycle**
> Visit mometrix.com/academy and enter code: 426578

LAYERS OF THE ATMOSPHERE

The **atmosphere** consists of 78% nitrogen, 21% oxygen, and 1% argon. It also includes traces of water vapor, carbon dioxide and other gases, dust particles, and chemicals from Earth. The atmosphere becomes thinner the farther it is from the Earth's surface. It becomes difficult to breathe at about 3 km above sea level. The atmosphere gradually fades into space.

The main layers of the Earth's atmosphere (from lowest to highest) are:

- **Troposphere** (lowest layer): where life exists and most weather occurs; elevation 0–15 km
- **Stratosphere**: has the ozone layer, which absorbs UV radiation; elevation 15–50 km
- **Mesosphere**: coldest layer; where meteors will burn up; elevation 50–80 km
- **Thermosphere**: where the international space station and most satellites orbit; hottest layer; elevation 80–600 km
- **Exosphere** (outermost layer): consists mainly of hydrogen and helium; extends to ~10,000 km

> **Review Video: Earth's Atmosphere**
> Visit mometrix.com/academy and enter code: 417614

TROPOSPHERIC CIRCULATION

Most weather takes place in the **troposphere**. Air circulates in the atmosphere by convection and in various types of "cells." Air near the equator is warmed by the Sun and rises. Cool air rushes under it, and the higher, warmer air flows toward Earth's poles. At the poles, it cools and descends to the surface. It is now under the hot air, and flows back to the equator. Air currents coupled with ocean currents move heat around the planet, creating winds, weather, and climate. Winds can change direction with the seasons. For example, in Southeast Asia and India, summer monsoons are caused by air being heated by the Sun. This air rises, draws moisture from the ocean, and causes daily rains. In winter, the air cools, sinks, pushes the moist air away, and creates dry weather.

WEATHER

Weather is the result of transfers of kinetic (heat) energy due to differences in temperature between objects as well as transfers of moisture in Earth's atmosphere. **Meteorology**, the study of weather, covers the same natural events as climatology, but observes them on a shorter time scale (usually no more than a few days). Rain, fog, snow, and wind are all examples of weather phenomena. The processes that occur at different stages in the hydrologic cycle form the basis of meteorological events. Most of the activity that produces the weather we experience on Earth takes place in the **troposphere**, the lowest level of the atmosphere. Atmospheric pressure, temperature, humidity, elevation, wind speed, and cloud cover are all factors in the study of weather.

OZONE LAYER

The **Earth's ozone layer** is the region of the stratosphere with a high concentration of ozone (a form of oxygen) particles. These molecules are formed through the process of **photolysis**, which occurs when ultraviolet light from the sun collides with oxygen molecules (O_2) in the atmosphere. The ultraviolet radiation splits the oxygen atoms apart; when a free oxygen atom strikes an oxygen molecule, it combines with the molecule to create an **ozone particle** (O_3). Ozone molecules may be broken down by interaction with nitrogen-, chlorine-, and hydrogen-containing compounds, or by thermal energy from the sun. Under normal conditions, these creative and destructive processes balance the levels of ozone in the stratosphere. The concentration of ozone molecules in the atmosphere absorbs ultraviolet radiation, thus preventing this harmful energy from reaching the Earth's surface. Ozone particles form in the region of the atmosphere over the equator, which receives the most direct sunlight. Atmospheric winds then disperse the particles throughout the rest of the stratosphere.

AIR MASS

An **air mass** is a body of air that exhibits consistent temperatures and levels of moisture throughout. These (usually large) pockets of air tend to come together under relatively still conditions, where air can remain in one place long enough to adopt the temperature and moisture characteristics of the land below it; this often occurs above wide areas of flat land. The region in which an air mass originates and the course of its motion are used to name it. For example, a maritime tropical air mass (denoted mT) is formed over the Gulf of Mexico (a tropical climate) and moves across the Atlantic Ocean (a maritime area). The conditions of an air mass will remain constant as long as the body is still, but when it moves across surfaces with different conditions, it may adopt those qualities. For example, polar air that moves over tropical land areas will be heated by the conditions below. Generally, maritime air masses contain high levels of moisture, and continental air masses are drier.

METEOROLOGICAL DEPRESSION

A **meteorological depression** refers to a **low-pressure zone** (created by rising air) situated between 30- and 60-degrees latitude. These zones vary from approximately 321–3,218 kilometers in diameter. The rising air associated with a depression usually condenses at higher levels in the atmosphere and causes precipitation. Depressions are formed when warm air masses and cold air masses converge. At first, a single front (boundary between converging masses of air with different temperatures) separates the air masses.

A distortion similar to the crest of a water wave develops, creating a small center of low pressure. Then, differentiated warm and cold fronts develop from that center. A mass of warm air forms and rises over the body of cold air. The cold front and the cold air eventually catch up with the warm air, creating an occluded front and causing pressure to rise, effectually slowing the depression's movement. Depressions usually have life spans of four to seven days.

PREVAILING WINDS AND WIND BELTS

Wind (the horizontal movement of air with respect to Earth's surface) forms due to pressure gradients (differences) in the atmosphere. Air tends to move from areas of **high pressure** (such as the poles) to areas of **low pressure** (such as the tropics). Prevailing winds, or trade winds, are the winds (named in meteorology for the direction they come from) that blow most frequently in a particular region. For instance, the prevailing winds most common in the region from 90 to 60 degrees north latitude blow from the northeast, and are generally called the Polar Easterlies. Wind belts are created in areas where prevailing winds converge with other prevailing winds or air masses. The Inter-Tropical Convergence Zone (ITCZ), where air coming from tropical areas north and south of the equator come together, is an example of a wind belt.

> **Review Video: Where Does Wind Come From?**
> Visit mometrix.com/academy and enter code: 451712

CORIOLIS FORCE

The **Coriolis force**, which gives rise to the **Coriolis effect**, is not really a force at all. Rather, it appears to be there to us because the Earth is a rotating frame of reference and we are inside it. In the atmosphere, air tends to move from areas of high pressure to areas of lower pressure. This air would move in a straight line but for the Coriolis force, which appears to deflect the air and cause it to **swirl**. Really, however, the Earth moves underneath the wind, which creates the impression of swirling air to someone standing on the Earth's surface. The Coriolis force causes winds to swing to the right as they approach the Northern Hemisphere and to the left as they approach the Southern Hemisphere.

AIR STABILITY IN THE ATMOSPHERE

Air stability is the tendency for air to rise or fall through the atmosphere under its own power. Heated air rises because it is less dense than the surrounding air. As a pocket of air rises, however, it will expand and become cooler with changes in atmospheric pressure. If the ambient air into which rising air ascends does not cool as quickly with altitude as the rising air does, that air will rapidly become cooler (and heavier) than the surrounding air and descend back to its original position. The air in this situation is said to be stable. However, if the air into which the warm pocket rises becomes colder with increased altitude, the warm air will continue its ascent. In this case, the air is unstable. Unstable air conditions (such as those that exist in depressions) lead to the formation of large clouds of precipitation.

CLOUDS

The four main **types of clouds** are cirrus, cumulous, nimbus, and stratus. A **cirrus** cloud forms high in a stable atmosphere, generally at altitudes of 6,000 meters or higher. Temperatures at these altitudes (in the troposphere) decrease with increased altitude; therefore, the precipitation in a cirrus cloud adopts the form of ice crystals. These usually thin traces of clouds may indicate an approaching weather depression. A cumulous cloud is a stereotypical white, fluffy ball. **Cumulous** clouds are indicators of a stable atmosphere, and also of the vertical extent of convection in the atmosphere—condensation and cloud formation begin at the flat base of a cumulous cloud. The more humid the air, the lower a cumulous cloud will form. A **nimbus** cloud is, generally speaking, a rain cloud. Nimbus clouds are usually low, dark, and formless, sometimes spanning the entire visible sky. A **stratus** cloud is basically a cloud of fog which forms at a distance above the Earth's surface. This type of cloud forms when weak convective currents bring moisture just high enough to initiate condensation (if the temperature is below the dew point).

The four cloud subtypes are cumulonimbus, cirrostratus, altocumulus, and stratocumulus. A **cumulonimbus** cloud is produced by rapid convection in unstable air. This type of cloud (which is often dark) is formed as a large, tall "tower." Collections of these towers (squall lines) often signal a coming cold front. Thunderstorms often involve cumulonimbus clouds. A **cirrostratus** cloud is an ultra-thin formation with a white tint and a transparent quality. An **altocumulus** cloud forms at an altitude from 1,980 to 6,100 meters. Clouds of this type, which appear to be flattened spheres, often form in clumps, waves, or lines. A **stratocumulus** cloud forms as a globular mass or flake. Stratocumulus clouds usually come together in layers or clumps.

> **Review Video: Clouds**
> Visit mometrix.com/academy and enter code: 803166

LIGHTNING

Lightning is a natural electrostatic discharge that produces light and releases electromagnetic radiation. It is believed that the separation of positive and negative charge carriers within a cloud is achieved by the polarization mechanism. The first step of this mechanism occurs when falling precipitation particles become **electrically polarized** after they move through the Earth's magnetic field. The second step of the polarization mechanism involves **electrostatic induction**, the process whereby electrically charged particles create charges in other particles without direct contact. Ice particles are charged though this method, and then energy-storing electric fields are formed between the charged particles. The positively-charged ice crystals tend to rise to the top of the

93

cloud, effectively polarizing the cloud with positive charges on top and negative charges at the middle and bottom. When charged clouds conglomerate, an electric discharge (a lightning bolt) is produced, either between clouds or between a cloud and the Earth's surface.

THUNDERSTORMS

A **thunderstorm** is a weather phenomenon that includes lightning, thunder, and usually large amounts of precipitation and strong winds. Thunder is the noise made by the rapid expansion and contraction of air due to the heat energy produced by lightning bolts. A thunderstorm develops when heating on the Earth's surface causes large amounts of air to rise into an unstable atmosphere. This results in large clouds of rain and ice crystals. The associated condensation releases high levels of heat, which in turn power the growth cycle of the cloud. The clouds created during thunderstorms are immense, sometimes reaching widths of several miles and extending to heights of 10,000 meters or more. The precipitation in such clouds eventually becomes heavy enough to fall against the updraft of unstable air; the consequent downpour is often short but intense. The differential speeds at which light and sound travel through the atmosphere enable one to estimate the distance between oneself and the storm by observing the interval between a lightning bolt and a thunderclap.

HURRICANES

Hurricanes form when several conditions are met: Oceanic water must be at least 26 degrees Celsius, the general circulation pattern of wind must be disrupted (this disruption usually takes the form of an atmospheric wave in the easterly trade winds), and the Coriolis force must be in effect. During hurricane season (June to November), easterly waves appear in the trade winds every few days. When such a wave occurs over a body of particularly warm, deep water, it is strengthened by the evaporation of warm air from below. Surrounding winds converge at the low-pressure zone created by the wave; air brought by these winds rises because it has nowhere else to go. The large body of warm, moist air rises high into the atmosphere and consequently condenses into huge clouds. As more and more humid air is drawn upward, this air begins to rotate around the area of low pressure. The storm continues to gain strength and may move toward land.

> **Review Video: Tornadoes**
> Visit mometrix.com/academy and enter code: 540439

EL NINO

El Niño refers to the **unusual warming of surface waters** near the equatorial coast of South America. This phenomenon occurs during the winter approximately every two to seven years, lasting from a few weeks to a few months. El Nino can cause torrential rains, violent winds, drought, and dangerously high temperatures in surrounding areas. El Nino is caused by a reversal of the atmospheric pressures on the eastern and western sides of the Pacific (normally, pressure is high on the eastern side near South America and lower on the western side near the Indonesian coast). This reversal causes a wave of warm water to flow eastward and sea levels to fall on the western side. The changes in air pressure and ocean temperature cause moisture levels in the western Pacific to rise drastically while the region east of the Pacific experiences drought. The air pressure changes also weaken the region's trade winds, which normally serve to distribute heat and moisture.

MONSOONS AND SAVANNAHS

The term **monsoon** refers to a unique pattern of moving air and currents that occurs when winds reverse direction with a change in season. India and Southeast Asia experience the most intense monsoons. This area lies between tropical and subtropical climate zones. During the winter season, northeasterly winds (which are generally dry) move from high-pressure subtropical areas to lower-pressure tropical areas. During the summer season, the continents of India and Asia heat up, creating a low-pressure zone. This causes winds to reverse and blow southwesterly across the Indian Ocean, accumulating high levels of moisture, thereby creating large amounts of precipitation during this season.

Savannahs also exist between wet equatorial and dry subtropical climate zones. These regions are characterized by vegetation consisting mainly of shrubs and grass. Savannahs experience dry weather throughout most of the year. A single, brief rainy season that occurs when the Sun is directly above the region interrupts prolonged dry spells.

INFLUENCE OF MOUNTAINS ON CLIMATE

At the level of local climate, the presence of mountains forces air to rise to travel above them; this contributes to increased formation of clouds and consequently, increases in levels of precipitation. Mountain chains can affect regional and even global climates by deflecting airflow. The Coriolis force causes most of Earth's atmospheric airflow to move east and west. Therefore, the presence of north-south–oriented mountain chains can alter general circulation patterns. For example, the Rocky Mountains force air to move northward; the air cools near the North Pole before blowing back down. This causes winter temperatures in Canada and parts of the United States to be very cold.

HUMIDITY AND CLOUD COVER

Humidity is a measure of the amount of water vapor in the air. **Specific humidity** is the expression of humidity as a ratio of aqueous vapor to dry air; it is expressed as a ratio of mass of water vapor per unit mass of natural (dry) air. **Absolute humidity** measures the mass of water vapor in a given volume of moist air or gas; it is expressed in grams per cubic foot or per cubic meter. The equilibrium (or saturated) vapor pressure of a gas is the vapor pressure (created by the movement of molecules) of water vapor when air is saturated with water vapor. **Relative humidity**, usually expressed as a percentage, is the ratio of the vapor pressure of water in air (or another gas) to the equilibrium vapor pressure. In other words, it is a ratio of the mass of water per volume of gas and the mass per volume of a saturated gas. Cloud cover refers to the amount of sky blocked by clouds at a given location.

MEASURING WEATHER

Weather can be measured by a variety of methods. The simplest include measurement of rainfall, sunshine, pressure, humidity, temperature, and cloudiness with basic instruments such as thermometers, barometers, and rain gauges. However, the use of radar (which involves analysis of microwaves reflecting off of raindrops) and satellite imagery grants meteorologists a look at the big picture of weather across, for example, an entire continent. This helps them understand and make predictions about current and developing weather systems. Infrared (heat-sensing) imaging allows meteorologists to measure the temperature of clouds above ground. Using weather reports gathered from different weather stations spread over an area, meteorologists create synoptic charts. The locations and weather reports of several stations are plotted on a chart; analysis of the pressures reported from each location, as well as rainfall, cloud cover, and so on, can reveal basic weather patterns.

GLOBAL WARMING

The **natural greenhouse effect** of the atmosphere is beneficial to life on Earth; it keeps temperatures on the planet 33 degrees higher than they would be without this phenomenon. Originally, this helped sustain life. However, it has been discovered in the last 20 years that this effect is being intensified by the actions of humans. In the twentieth century, certain activities of mankind, including the burning of fossils fuels like coal and oil, have resulted in an **increase in the levels of greenhouse gases** (such as methane and carbon dioxide) being released into the atmosphere. Also, increasing deforestation has affected the number of photosynthesis-practicing plants. The combined effect of these trends is a higher-than-normal concentration of greenhouse gases in the atmosphere. This, in turn, produces the effect of global warming. The average temperature at the Earth's surface has gone up 0.6 degrees Celsius in the last 100 years. Continuation of this trend is likely to have a detrimental effect on many of the planet's ecosystems, including that of human beings.

Space Science

EARTH'S ROTATION

The **Earth rotates** west to east about its axis, an imaginary straight line that runs nearly vertically through the center of the planet. This rotation (which takes 23 hours, 56 minutes, and 5 seconds) places each section of the Earth's surface in a position facing the Sun for a period of time, thus creating the alternating periods of light and darkness we experience as **day and night**. This rotation constitutes a sidereal day; it is measured as the amount of time required for a reference star to cross the meridian (an imaginary north-south line above an observer). Each star crosses the meridian once every (sidereal) day. Since the speed at which Earth rotates is not exactly constant, we use the mean solar day (a 24-hour period) in timekeeping rather than the slightly variable sidereal day.

SUN

The **Sun** is the vital force of life on Earth; it is also the central component of our solar system. It is basically a sphere of extremely hot gases (close to 15 million degrees at the core) held together by gravity. Some of these gaseous molecules are ionized due to the high temperatures. The balance between its gravitational force and the pressure produced by the hot gases is called **hydrostatic equilibrium**. The source of the solar energy that keeps the Sun alive and plays a key role in the perpetuation of life on Earth is located in the Sun's core, where nucleosynthesis produces heat energy and photons. The Sun's atmosphere consists of the photosphere, the surface visible from Earth, the chromosphere, a layer outside of and hotter than the photosphere, the transition zone (the region where temperatures rise between the chromosphere and the corona), and the corona, which is best viewed at x-ray wavelengths. A solar flare is an explosive emission of ionized particles from the Sun's surface.

> **Review Video: The Sun**
> Visit mometrix.com/academy and enter code: 699233

EARTH'S REVOLUTION AROUND THE SUN

Like all celestial objects in our solar system, planet Earth revolves around the Sun. This process takes approximately 365 1/4 days, the period of time that constitutes a calendar year. The path of the orbit of Earth around the Sun is not circular but **elliptical**. Therefore, the distances between the Earth and the Sun at points on either extreme of this counterclockwise orbit are not equal. In other words, the distance between the two objects varies over the course of a year. At **perihelion**, the minimum heliocentric distance, Earth is 147 million kilometers from the Sun. At **aphelion**, the maximum heliocentric distance, Earth is 152 million kilometers from the Sun. This movement of the

Earth is responsible for the apparent annual motions of the Sun (in a path referred to as the ecliptic) and other celestial objects visible from Earth's surface.

Review Video: <u>Astronomy</u>
Visit mometrix.com/academy and enter code: 640556

Review Video: <u>Solar System</u>
Visit mometrix.com/academy and enter code: 273231

SEASONS

The combined effects of Earth's revolution around the Sun and the tilt of the planet's rotational axis create the **seasons**. Earth's axis is not perfectly perpendicular to its orbital plane; rather, it is **tilted** about 23.5 degrees. Thus, at different times of the year, certain areas of the surface receive different amounts of sunlight. For example, during the period of time in Earth's orbit when the Northern Hemisphere is tipped toward the Sun, it is exposed to higher amounts of nearly direct sunlight than at any other time of year (days are longer, and the direction of Sun's rays striking the surface is nearly perpendicular). This period of time is summer in the Northern Hemisphere and winter in the Southern Hemisphere; on the opposite side of the orbit, the seasons are reversed in each hemisphere.

Review Video: <u>Earth's Tilt and Seasons</u>
Visit mometrix.com/academy and enter code: 602892

SUMMER AND WINTER SOLSTICES

The **summer solstice** occurs when Earth's orbital position and axial tilt point the North Pole most directly toward the Sun. This happens on or near June 21 each year. On this day in the Northern Hemisphere, the Sun appears to be directly overhead (at its zenith) at 12:00 noon. The entire Arctic Circle (the north polar region above approximately 66.5 degrees north latitude) is bathed in sunlight for a complete solar day. The North Pole itself experiences constant daylight for six full months. Conversely, the **winter solstice** occurs when the South Pole is oriented most directly toward the Sun. This phenomenon, which falls on or near December 22 each year, orients the Sun as viewed from the Northern Hemisphere at its lowest point above the horizon.

EQUINOXES

The **ecliptic** (the Sun's apparent path through the sky) crosses Earth's equatorial plane twice during the year; these intersections occur when the North Pole is at a right angle from the line connecting the Earth and the Sun. At these times, the two hemispheres experience equal periods of light and dark. These two points in time are respectively referred to as the vernal (spring) equinox (on or about March 21) and the autumnal (fall) equinox (on or about September 23). A calendar year is measured as the length of time between vernal equinoxes.

MOON

Earth's Moon is historically one of the most studied celestial bodies. Its mass is approximately 1.2% of the Earth's mass, and its radius is just over one-fourth of the size of the Earth's radius. Measurements of the Moon's density suggest that its characteristics are similar to those of the rocks that make up Earth's crust. The **landscape** of the Moon consists mostly of mountains and craters formed by collisions of this surface with meteors and other interplanetary materials. The Moon's crust (estimated to be 50 to 100 kilometers in thickness) is made up of a layer of regolith (lunar soil) supported by a layer of loose rocks and gravel. Beneath the crust is a mantle made up of a solid lithosphere and a semiliquid asthenosphere. The Moon's **core** (the innermost 500 kilometers of the body) is not as dense as that of the Earth. The Moon is made up mostly of refractory elements with high melting and boiling points with low levels of heavy elements such as iron.

FORMATION THEORIES

The **fission model** of Moon origin suggests that the Moon is actually a piece of the Earth that split off early during the planet's formation. In this model, a portion of the Earth's mantle fissioned off during a liquid stage in its formation, creating the Moon. According to the **capture model**, the Moon formed elsewhere in the solar system and was subsequently captured by the Earth's gravitational field. The **double-impact model** states that the Earth and the Moon formed during the same period of time from the same accretion material. Each of these theories has its strengths, but none of them can explain all of the properties of the Moon and its relationship to the Earth. Recently, a fourth (widely accepted) hypothesis has been suggested, which involves the **collision** between the Earth and a large asteroid. This hypothetical collision is said to have released a large amount of Earth's crustal material into its orbit; the Moon accreted from that material and the material displaced from the asteroid due to the collision.

EARTH-MOON SYSTEM

While the Moon is commonly referred to as a satellite of the Earth, this is not entirely accurate. The ratio of the masses of the two bodies is much larger than that of any other planet-satellite system. Also, the Moon does not truly **revolve** around the Earth. Rather, the two bodies revolve around a common center of mass beneath the surface of the Earth (approximately 4,800 kilometers from Earth's core). The **orbital planes** of the Moon and the Earth are nearly aligned; therefore, the Moon moves close to the ecliptic, as seen from Earth. Due to the Moon's synchronous rotation (its rotation period and orbital period are equal); the same side of the Moon is always facing Earth. This occurs because of the **mutual gravitational** pull between the two bodies.

PHASES

The **sidereal period** of the Moon (the time it takes the Moon to orbit the Earth with the fixed stars as reference points) is about 27 days. The **lunar month** (or synodic period) is the period of time required for the Moon to return to a given alignment as observed from the Earth with the Sun as a reference point; this takes 29 days, 12 hours, 44 minutes, and 28 seconds. A discrepancy exists between the two periods of time because the Earth and the Moon move at the same time. Sunlight reflected off of the Moon's surface at different times during the lunar month causes its apparent shape to change. The sequence of the Moon's shapes is referred to as the **phases of the Moon**. The full Moon can be viewed when the body is directly opposite from the Sun. The opposite end of the cycle, the new Moon, occurs when the Moon is not visible from Earth because it is situated between the Earth and the Sun.

CONFIGURATIONS

The **configurations of the Moon** describe its position with respect to the Earth and the Sun. We can thus observe a correlation between the phases of the Moon and its configuration. The Moon is at **conjunction** at the time of the new Moon—it is situated in the same direction as the Sun. **Quadrature** (which signals the first quarter phase) is the position of the Moon at a right angle between the Earth-Sun line; we see exactly half of the Moon's sunlit hemisphere. This is the **waxing crescent phase**, in which we see more of the Moon each night. Then comes opposition (which occurs when the Moon lies in the direction opposite the Sun)—we see the full Moon. After this point, the Moon enters its **waning gibbons phase** as it travels back toward quadrature. When it reaches that point again, it has entered the third-quarter phase. Finally, as the Moon circles back toward conjunction, it is in its waning crescent phase.

TERRESTRIAL PLANETS

The term **terrestrial planets** refers to the four planets closest to the Sun (Mercury, Venus, Earth, and Mars). They are classified together because they share many similarities that distinguish them from the giant planets. The terrestrial planets have **high densities and atmospheres** that constitute a small percentage of their total masses. These atmospheres consist mostly of heavy elements, such as carbon dioxide, nitrogen, and water, and are maintained by the gravitational field of the planets (which could not prevent hydrogen from escaping). These planets exhibit magnetic fields of varying intensity. An important characteristic that distinguishes the terrestrial planets from the giant planets is the evidence of various levels of internally generated activity, which caused these planets to evolve from their original states. These processes are thought to have been caused by constant meteoritic impacts during the first few hundred million years of the planets' existence. Radioactive decay of certain isotopes increased the internal temperatures of these planets, leading to volcanic activity on all of the terrestrial planets except Venus.

> **Review Video: Terrestrial Planets**
> Visit mometrix.com/academy and enter code: 100346

MERCURY

Mercury, the smallest interior planet, is the least well known of the four. This is due to its close proximity to the Sun and high temperatures. Mercury's atmosphere is not very dense; this means that the planet's surface experiences wide temperature differentials from day to night. Mercury's density is close to that of Earth. As the smallest planet known to have experienced planetary evolution, Mercury's internal activity ceased (it became extinct) thousands of millions of years ago. The size of the planet is relevant because less massive bodies cool more quickly than larger ones after cessation of radioactivity. Mercury's surface is characterized by craters produced by meteoritic impact.

VENUS

Venus is comparable to Earth in both mass and density. Venus is the brightest planet in the sky (partially due to the fact that it is proximate to the Sun), which makes exploration of its surface difficult. This planet's atmosphere consists mainly of carbon dioxide, with trace amounts of water and carbon oxide molecules, as well as high levels of sulfuric, nitric, and hydrofluoric acids in the clouds that characterize this atmosphere. The concentration of clouds, coupled with the chemical makeup of Venus's atmosphere, result in a strong greenhouse effect at the planet's surface. This surface consists of large plains (thought to be created by either volcanic activity, which remains unproven, or by meteoritic impacts) and large impact craters. The materials that compose Venus's surface are highly radioactive. Some astronomers have suggested past single-plate tectonic activity; again, however, the planet's dense atmosphere makes valid surface observation quite difficult.

MARS

Mars and Earth exhibit many similarities. For example, Mars has an internal structure that includes a central metallic core, a mantle rich in olivine and iron oxide, and a crust of hydrated silicates. Martian soil consists largely of basalts and clay silicate, with elements of sulfur, silicon oxide, and iron oxide. The planet's surface belies high levels of past volcanic activity (though, due to its relatively small mass, it is probably extinct). In fact, Mars is home to the largest known volcano in the solar system. The Martian landscape also includes two major basins, ridges and plateaus, and, most notably, apparent evidence of fluvial (water-based) erosion landforms, such as canyons and canals. It is possible that the past pressures and temperatures on Mars allowed water to exist on the red planet. Some have gone so far as to suggest that this planet was a site of biochemical evolution. So far, however, no evidence of life has been found.

MARS'S SATELLITES

Two Martian satellites have been observed: **Phobos** and **Deimos**. Each of these bodies is ellipsoidal; the circular orbits of the two satellites lie in Mars's equatorial plane. The gravitational forces between this planet and Phobos and Deimos have caused both satellites to settle into synchronous rotation (the same parts of their surfaces are always facing Mars). This feature exerts a braking force on Phobos's orbit. In other words, its orbit is decreasing in size. The relationship between Deimos and Mars is similar to the Earth-Moon system, in which the radius of the satellite's orbit is gradually growing. The differential compositions and densities of Mars and its satellites indicate that Phobos and Deimos probably did not break off from Mars.

GIANT PLANETS

The **large diameters** of Jupiter, Saturn, Uranus, and Neptune gave rise to the name of the category into which they fall. The **hypothetical icy cores** of these planets cause them to exhibit primary atmospheres, because the large levels of mass they accreted prevented even the lightest elements from escaping their gravitational pulls. The atmospheres of the giant planets thus consist mostly of hydrogen and helium. The giant planets do not have solid surfaces like those of the terrestrial planets. Jupiter probably consists of a core (made of ice and rock) surrounded by a layer of metallic hydrogen, which is covered by a convective atmosphere of hydrogen and helium. Saturn is believed to have the same type of core and hydrogen mantle, enriched by the helium missing from the atmosphere, surrounded by a differentiation zone and a hydrogenic atmosphere. Uranus and Neptune probably have the same type of core, surrounded by ionic materials, bounded by methane-rich molecular envelopes. Uranus is the only giant planet that exhibits no evidence of internal activity.

RINGS

Each of the four giant planets exhibits **rings**. These are flat disks of fragmented material that orbit just next to their respective planets. Many of the giant planets' smaller satellites are embedded in these rings. There are two main hypotheses regarding the formation of such rings. One theory suggests that the tidal force exerted on a satellite by its planet may surpass the **Roche limit** (the point at which particle cohesion is no longer possible) and break the satellite into fragments, which then collide and become smaller. This material then spreads out and forms a ring. An alternate theory of the formation of the rings of the giant planets suggests that there was unaccreted material left over after the formation of these planets. Below the Roche limit (within a certain vicinity to the planet), these particles could not join together to form satellites and would consequently settle into orbital rings.

SATELLITES

Each of the giant planets possesses a number of **satellites**. **Jupiter** has over 50 known satellites—they are grouped according to size. Each of the four largest satellites of Jupiter exhibits evidence of internal activity at some point in their evolutions. In fact, Io, the densest satellite and the one closest to Jupiter, is the only celestial body besides Earth known to be currently volcanically active. **Saturn** has 21 satellites. Titan, the second-largest known satellite, has its own atmosphere. The other six largest of Saturn's satellites all have icy surfaces; some of these show evidence of past internal activity. The smaller 14 are relatively unknown. **Uranus** has five satellites. Each of them displays evidence of geological activity, in the form of valleys, smoothed surfaces, cliffs, mountains, and depressions. **Neptune** has eight known satellites. The larger, Triton, is similar to Titan in that it has an atmosphere. The other seven satellites of Neptune are relatively unknown.

PLUTO AND CHARON

Though **Charon** was originally considered a satellite of Pluto, the ninth planet in the solar system, it now appears that the two are more accurately described as a **double-planet system** (largely because of the similarity in the sizes of the two). It is believed that these bodies formed from the solar nebula like most other objects in the solar system. Pluto has a highly irregular orbit, which places it closer to the Sun than Neptune for periods of time. In sharp contrast to its giant neighbors, this planet's density is higher than that of water ice. The surface of Pluto consists of high levels of methane absorbed into ice, with trace amounts of carbon oxide and nitrogen. Charon resembles the major Uranian satellites more so than it does Pluto. It consists of water ice with a siliceous or hydrocarbonate contaminant.

KEPLER'S LAWS

Kepler's laws are a collection of observations about the motion of planets in the solar system. Formulated by Johannes Kepler in the 1600s, these laws are still vital to our understanding of the way the universe works. **Kepler's first law** states that each planet moves in its own elliptical path and that all of these orbits have the Sun as their singular focal point. Before Kepler's discovery, astronomers had assumed that planetary orbits were circular (because the heavens were assumed to be geometrically perfect). **Kepler's second law** says that a straight line between a planet and the Sun sweeps out equal areas in equal time. In other words, planets move quickest in the part of their orbit that is closest to the Sun, and vice versa. **Kepler's third law** states that the further a planet is from the Sun, the longer its orbital period will be. In mathematical terms, the square of a planet's period is inversely proportional to the cube of the radius of its orbit.

STELLAR OBSERVATION

The observation of stars relates to one of three stellar properties: position, brightness, and spectra. **Positional stellar observation** is principally performed through study of the positions of stars on multiple photographic plates. Historically, this type of analysis was done through measurement of the angular positions of the stars in the sky. **Parallax** of a star is its apparent shift in position due to the revolution of the Earth about the Sun; this property can be used to establish the distance to a star. Observation of the **brightness** of a star involves the categorization of stars according to their magnitudes. There is a fixed intensity ratio between each of the six magnitudes. Since stars emit light over a range of wavelengths, viewing a star at different wavelengths can give an indication of its temperature. The analysis of stars' **spectra** provides information about the temperatures of stars—the higher a star's temperature, the more ionized the gas in its outer layer. A star's spectrum also relates to its chemical composition.

BINARY STAR

Binary star systems, of which about fifty percent of the stars in the sky are members, consist of two stars that orbit each other. The orbits of and distances between members of a binary system vary. A **visual binary** is a pair of stars that can be visually observed. Positional measurements of a visual binary reveal the orbital paths of the two stars. Astronomers can identify astrometric binaries through long-term observation of a visible star—if the star appears to wobble, it may be inferred that it is orbiting a companion star that is not visible. An **eclipsing binary** can be identified through observation of the brightness of a star. Variations in the visual brightness of a star can occur when one star in a binary system passes in front of the other. Sometimes, variations in the spectral lines of a star occur because it is in a binary system. This type of binary is a spectroscopic binary.

> **Review Video: Types of Stars**
> Visit mometrix.com/academy and enter code: 831934

HERTZSPRUNG-RUSSELL DIAGRAM

The **Hertzsprung-Russell (H-R) diagram** was developed to explore the relationships between the luminosities and spectral qualities of stars. This diagram involves plotting these qualities on a graph, with absolute magnitude (luminosity) on the vertical and spectral class on the horizontal. Plotting a number of stars on the H-R diagram demonstrates that stars fall into narrowly defined regions, which correspond to stages in stellar evolution. Most stars are situated in a diagonal strip that runs from the top-left (high temperature, high luminosity) to the lower-right (low temperature, low luminosity). This diagonal line shows stars in the main sequence of evolution (often called dwarfs). Stars that fall above this line on the diagram (low temperature, high luminosity) are believed to be much larger than the stars on the main sequence (because their high luminosities are not due to higher temperatures than main sequence stars); they are termed giants and supergiants. Stars below the main sequence (high temperature, low luminosity) are called white dwarfs. The H-R diagram is useful in calculating distances to stars.

STELLAR EVOLUTION

The life cycle of a star is closely related to its **mass**—low-mass stars become white dwarfs, while high-mass stars become **supernovae**. A star is born when a **protostar** is formed from a **collapsing interstellar cloud**. The temperature at the center of the protostar rises, allowing nucleosynthesis to begin. **Nucleosynthesis**, or hydrogen-burning through fusion, entails a release of energy. Eventually, the star runs out of fuel (hydrogen). If the star is relatively low mass, the disruption of hydrostatic equilibrium allows the star to contract due to gravity. This raises the temperature just outside the core to a point at which nucleosynthesis and a different kind of fusion (with helium as fuel) that produces a carbon nucleus can occur. The star swells with greater energy, becoming a red giant. Once this phase is over, gravity becomes active again, shrinking the star until the degeneracy pressure of electrons begins to operate, creating a white dwarf that will eventually burn out. If the star has a high mass, the depletion of hydrogen creates a supernova.

SUPERNOVA

When a star on the main sequence runs out of hydrogen fuel, it begins to burn helium (the by-product of nucleosynthesis). Once helium-burning is complete in a massive star, the mass causes the core temperature to rise, enabling the fusion of carbon, then silicon, and a succession of other atomic nuclei, each of which takes place in a new shell further out of the core. When the fusion cycle reaches iron (which cannot serve as fuel for a nuclear reaction), an iron core begins to form, which accumulates over time. Eventually, the temperature and pressure in the core become high enough for electrons to interact with protons in the iron nuclei to produce neutrons. In a matter of moments, this reaction is complete. The core falls and collides with the star's outer envelope, causing a massive explosion (a supernova). This continues until the neutrons exert degeneracy pressure; this creates a pulsar. In more massive stars, nothing can stop the collapse, which ends in the creation of a black hole.

METEOROID

A **meteoroid** is a small, solid fragment of material in the solar system. An enormous number of these objects are present in the system. The term meteor is used to refer to such a body when it enters the Earth's atmosphere. Interaction (friction) between meteors and the upper levels of the atmosphere cause them to break up; most disintegrate before they reach the surface. The heat associated with frictional forces causes meteors to glow, creating the phenomena of shooting stars. The meteors that are large enough to avoid complete disintegration, and can therefore travel all the way down through the atmosphere to Earth's surface, are termed meteorites. Analysis of these fragments indicates that these bodies originate from the Moon, Mars, comets, and small asteroids that cross Earth's orbital path. The forceful impacts of meteorites on Earth's surface compress, heat, and vaporize some of the materials of the meteorite as well as crustal materials, producing gases and water vapor.

ASTEROID

An **asteroid** is a small, solid planet (planetoid) that orbits the Sun. The orbital paths of most asteroids are between the orbits of Jupiter and Mars. Many of these bodies have been studied extensively and given names; those in the main belt (which tend to be carbonaceous) are classified into subgroups based on their distance from a large, named asteroid (for example, Floras, Hildas, Cybeles). **Atens** are asteroids whose orbits lie between the Earth and the Sun, and Apollos are asteroids with orbits that mimic Earth's. Asteroids may also be classified based on their composition. **C-type** asteroids exhibit compositions similar to that of the Sun and are fairly dark. S-type asteroids are made up of nickel-iron and iron- and magnesium-silicates; these are relatively bright. **Bright asteroids** made up exclusively of nickel-iron are classified as M-type. Observation of the relative brightness of an asteroid allows astronomers to estimate its size.

INTERSTELLAR MEDIUM

The **interstellar**, or interplanetary, **medium** (the space between planets and stars) is populated by comets, asteroids, and meteoroids. However, particles exist in this medium on an even smaller scale. Tiny solid bodies (close to a millionth of a meter in diameter) are called **interplanetary dust**. The accumulation of this material in arctic lakes, for example, allows scientists to study it. Such analysis has revealed that these grains are most likely miniscule fragments of the **nuclei of dead comets**. They possess low density, for they are really many microscopic particles stuck together. The interplanetary dust refracts sunlight, which produces a visible (but faint) glow in parts of the sky populated by clouds of this dust. The interstellar medium also contains particle remnants of **dead stars** and **gases** (such as hydrogen molecules ionized by ultraviolet photons). **Black holes** (objects that collapse under their own gravitational forces), which trap photons, are also believed to populate the interstellar medium. Black holes are a form of dark matter.

DARK MATTER

Observations of the **gravitational force** in the solar system (based on Kepler's laws) have indicated for years that there are bodies in the system that we cannot see. **Dark matter** (sometimes called missing matter) is thought to account for the unseen masses, though its exact nature is unknown. Some dark matter may simply be **ordinary celestial bodies** too small to be observed from Earth, even with technology such as high-powered telescopes. The presence of MACHOs (massive compact halo objects) has been noted through observation of distant galaxies—at certain times astronomers can discern dips in the brightness of these galaxies, thought to be caused by a large object (a MACHO) passing between Earth and the galaxy under observation. Some have postulated that dark matter is made up of **WIMPs** (weakly interacting massive particles), which do not interact with photons or other forms of electromagnetic radiation; these particles are hypothetical, because astronomers cannot detect or study them.

> **Review Video: Dark Matter**
> Visit mometrix.com/academy and enter code: 251909

ECLIPSES

Eclipses occur when one celestial body obscures the view of another, either partially or completely. A **solar eclipse**, or eclipse of the Sun by the Moon, happens when the Moon passes directly in front of the Sun (as observed from Earth). Alternately, a **lunar eclipse** occurs when the Moon is situated in the Earth's shadow and is therefore completely invisible. These events do not happen every month because of the differential between the orbital planes of the Moon and the Earth—the Moon's orbit is about five degrees off from the ecliptic. The Moon's orbital path is subject to the same precession that occurs in the Earth's rotational axis; this causes the occasional intersection of the orbital planes of the two bodies. Therefore, eclipses are produced by a combination of the effects of the precession of the Moon's orbit, the orbit itself, and the Earth's orbit.

> **Review Video: Eclipses**
> Visit mometrix.com/academy and enter code: 691598

NEWTON'S LAW OF GRAVITATION

Newton's law of gravitation (sometimes referred to as the law of universal gravitation) states that the force of gravity operates as an attractive force between all bodies in the universe. Prior to Newton's formulation of this law, scientists believed that two gravitational forces were at work in the universe—that gravity operated differently on Earth than it did in space. Newton's discovery served to unify these two conceptions of gravity. This law is expressed as a mathematical formula: $F = \frac{GMm}{D^2}$, in which F is the gravitational force, M and m are the masses of two bodies, D is the distance between them, and G is the gravitational constant ($6.67 \times 10^{-11} \frac{m^3}{kg\,s^2}$). The gravitational attraction between two objects, therefore, depends on the distance between them and their relative masses. Newton's law of gravitation served to clarify the mechanisms by which Kepler's laws operated. In effect, Newton proved Kepler's laws to be true through the development of this law.

> **Review Video: Newton's Law of Gravitation**
> Visit mometrix.com/academy and enter code: 709086

MILKY WAY

The **Milky Way**, which houses the Earth's solar system, is a spiral galaxy. It consists of a central bulging disk, the center of which is referred to as a **nucleus**. Most of a galaxy's visible light comes from stars in this region. The disk is surrounded by a halo of stars and star clusters that spread above, next to, and beneath the nucleus. **Globular clusters** (dense, spherical clusters of ancient stars) are often found in the halo. Spiral arms of high-luminosity stars (from which this type of galaxy gets its name) fan out from the nucleus as well, with stars that are less bright in between. Interstellar dust populates the entire galaxy between celestial bodies. The entire galaxy rotates about the center. While Earth, the Sun, and its solar system are located on the disk, we are far from the center of the Milky Way. The galaxy's mass is about 1.5 trillion solar masses.

STRUCTURES OF GALAXIES

Elliptical galaxies are roughly spherical. Within this category, subgroups based on the degree of flattening exhibited in the galaxy's shape range from E0 (spherical) to E7 (flat). A dwarf elliptical galaxy has a spheroidal shape, with low mass and low luminosity. An S0 galaxy is similar in shape to a spiral galaxy, but lacks spiral arms. Spiral galaxies such as the Milky Way are characterized by disk-like nuclei with spiral arms. Subtypes of this category are determined by the tightness of the spiral arms and the size of the nucleus; a spiral galaxy of Sa type has a large nucleus and tightly wound arms, and an Sc-type galaxy consists of a small nucleus with open spiral arms. A barred

Copyright © Mometrix Media. You have been licensed one copy of this document for personal use only. Any other reproduction or redistribution is strictly prohibited. All rights reserved.
This content is provided for test preparation purposes only and does not imply an endorsement by Mometrix of any particular political, scientific, or religious point of view.

spiral galaxy exhibits an elongated nucleus. The subtypes of barred spiral galaxies are determined like those of spiral galaxies. Some irregular galaxies (type I) display a loose spiral structure with high levels of disorganization. Other irregular galaxies (type II) can be of any shape.

MODEL OF THE INFLATIONARY UNIVERSE

Hubble's law states that the speed at which a galaxy appears to be moving away from the Earth is proportional to its distance from Earth. This relatively simple formula ($v = Hr$, where v is the **velocity of a receding galaxy**, r is its distance from Earth, and H is the Hubble constant) had an important implication at the time that it was developed—the universe is expanding. This fact, in turn, implies that the universe began at a **specific point** in the past. This model suggests that a random conglomeration of quarks and leptons, along with the strong force (all the forces in the universe unified as one), existed in the very dense, very hot, early universe. When the universe was a certain age (about 10–35 seconds old), the strong force separated out from the mass. This enabled the rapid expansion of the particles that formed the universe.

BIG BANG THEORY

The **theory of the big bang** expands upon the model of the **inflationary universe**. This theory hypothesizes that the early universe consisted of elementary particles, high energy density and high levels of pressure and heat. This single mass experienced a **phase change** (similar to that of freezing water) when it cooled and expanded. This transition caused the early universe to expand exponentially; this period of growth is called **cosmic inflation**. As it continued to grow, the temperature continued to fall. At some point, **baryogenesis** (an unknown process in which quarks and gluons become baryons, such as protons and neutrons) occurred, somehow creating the distinction between matter and antimatter. As the universe continued to cool, the **elementary forces** reached their present form, and **elementary particles** engaged in big bang **nucleosynthesis** (a process that produced helium and deuterium nuclei). **Gravity** became the predominant force governing interactions between particles; this enabled increasing accretion of particles of matter, which eventually formed the universal constituents as we recognize them today.

GACE Practice Test

Mathematics

1. The most effective way to structure a math session for the benefit of primary students is to:

    a. Check all homework assignments and be sure that all workbook pages are completed
    b. Focus almost entirely on computation skills
    c. Focus almost entirely on the application of math skills to real-life situations
    d. Divide class time evenly between computation skills and real-life applications

Refer to the following for question 2:

The box-and-whisker plot displays student test scores assessed throughout a semester to see if students were improving.

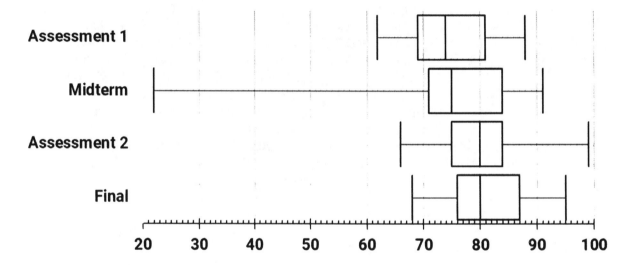

2. What is the probability that a test score chosen at random from the Final is less than 87?

    a. 0.25
    b. 0.5
    c. 0.6
    d. 0.75

3. Which of these relationships represents y as a function of x?

a. $x = y^4$ c. $y = |x - 2|$

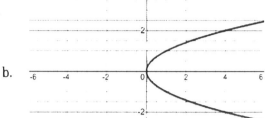 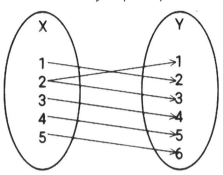

b.

d.

4. Which of these is a net of a triangular pyramid?

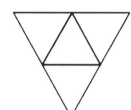

a.

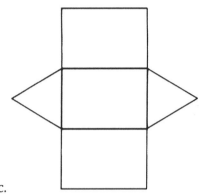

c.

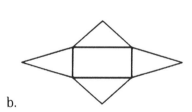

b.

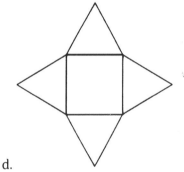

d.

5. Which of these approaches to mathematics instruction is generally recognized as being the most effective?

   a. Students need to memorize formulas and follow standard procedures for problem solving
   b. The use of mental math to solve complex problems should be discouraged
   c. Pencil-and-paper drills should be the primary focus of math class
   d. Students should be encouraged to solve problems in ways that make sense to them

6. Two coins are tossed. The probability of both coins landing as tails is 1 in:

   a. 2
   b. 3
   c. 4
   d. 8

7. Of 120 students who took an exam, 72 received a passing grade. What percent of the students failed the exam?

    a. 12%
    b. 40%
    c. 50%
    d. 60%

8. The simulation of a coin toss is completed 300 times. Which of the following best represents the number of tosses you can expect to show heads?

    a. 50
    b. 100
    c. 150
    d. 200

9. A parallelogram has sides measuring 8 inches, 3 inches, 8 inches, and 3 inches. What is the area of the parallelogram in square inches?

    a. 22
    b. 24
    c. 64
    d. Not enough information is given

10. A dress is marked down by 20% and placed on a clearance rack, on which is posted a sign reading, "Take an extra 25% off already reduced merchandise." What fraction of the original price is the final sale price of the dress?

    a. $\dfrac{2}{5}$
    b. $\dfrac{3}{5}$
    c. $\dfrac{9}{20}$
    d. $\dfrac{11}{20}$

11. A triangle with vertices $A(-4, -3)$, $B(-2, 0)$, and $C(-1, -1)$ is reflected across $y = x - 3$ to give $\Delta A'B'C'$, which is subsequently reflected across the y-axis to give $\Delta A''B''C''$. Which of these statements is true?

    a. A translation of ΔABC three units up gives $\Delta A''B''C''$.
    b. A reflection of ΔABC about the x-axis gives $\Delta A''B''C''$.
    c. A 90° rotation of ΔABC about $(0, -3)$ gives $\Delta A''B''C''$.
    d. A 270° rotation of ΔABC about $(0, -3)$ gives $\Delta A''B''C''$.

12. Jason decides to donate 1% of his annual salary to a local charity. If his annual salary is $45,000, how much will he donate?

    a. $4.50
    b. $45
    c. $450
    d. $4,500

13. Sara and her sister Kate are standing next to one another on the beach. Kate casts a shadow that is 32 inches long. Sara's shadow is 16 inches longer than her sister's. If Kate is 40 inches tall, how tall is Sara?

    a.   48 inches
    b.   52 inches
    c.   60 inches
    d.   Not enough information is given

14. Roxana walks x meters west and $x + 20$ meters south to get to her friend's house. On a neighborhood map which has a scale of 1 cm : 10 m, the direct distance between Roxana's house and her friend's house is 10 cm. How far did Roxana walk to her friend's house?

    a.   60 m
    b.   80 m
    c.   100 m
    d.   140 m

15. A dress is marked down 45%. The cost, after taxes, is $39.95. If the tax rate is 8.75%, what was the original price of the dress?

    a. $45.74
    b. $58.61
    c. $66.79
    d. $72.31

16. Solve the system of equations.

$$3x + 4y = 2$$
$$2x + 6y = -2$$

    a. $\left(0, \frac{1}{2}\right)$
    b. $\left(\frac{2}{5}, \frac{1}{5}\right)$
    c. $(2, -1)$
    d. $\left(-1, \frac{5}{4}\right)$

17. The first thing students should be encouraged to do when attempting to solve a mathematical word problem is to:

    a.   Write the appropriate equation
    b.   List the steps needed to solve the problem
    c.   Think about what information the problem is asking them to find
    d.   Compare the problem to similar problems they have solved in the past

18. The ratio of employee wages and benefits to all other operational costs of a business is 2 : 3. If a business's total operating expenses are $130,000 per month, how much money does the company spend on employee wages and benefits?

    a. $43,333.33
    b. $52,000.00
    c. $78,000.00
    d. $86,666.67

19. What is a true statement about the circles below?

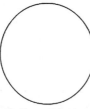
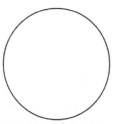

Radius = 8 inches   Radius = 12 inches

    a.   They are congruent.
    b.   They are similar.
    c.   They are neither congruent nor similar.
    d.   They are equal.

20. Levi walked to the grocery store and back. The graph below shows his distance from home at times throughout the walk. If the y-axis represents the distance from home in miles and the x-axis represents the number of hours he was gone, which of the following statements is (are) true?

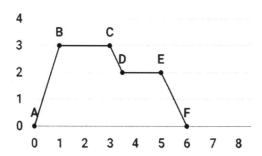

    I. Levi's average speed was 1 mph.
    II. Levi's speed from point A to point B was the same as from point E to F.
    III. Levi walked a total distance of six miles.

    a.   I only
    b.   II only
    c.   I and II
    d.   I and III

21. At Whiteley Elementary School, 60 percent of the 720 students are entering a nationwide essay contest. Which of the following computations can be used to determine how many students will be entering the contest?

    a. $720 \div 0.60$
    b. $\frac{3}{5} \times 720$
    c. $\frac{1}{60} \times 720$
    d. $720 - \frac{40}{100}$

22. Which of these could be the equation of the function graphed below?

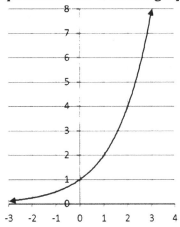

a. $f(x) = x^2$
b. $f(x) = \sqrt{x}$
c. $f(x) = 2^x$
d. $f(x) = \log_2 x$

23. What is the probability of drawing two consecutive aces from a deck of 52 cards?

a. 2/52
b. 1/104
c. 3/104
d. 1/221

Refer to the following for question 24:

The box-and-whisker plot displays a district's standardized test scores by subject.

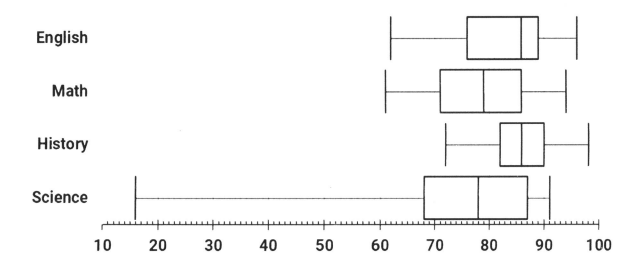

24. Which subject has the smallest range of test scores?

 a. English
 b. Math
 c. History
 d. Science

25. Four classes have raised money for charity. The amounts raised were $65, $88, $94, and $110. What is the median amount raised by the four classes?

 a. $89.50
 b. $91
 c. $110
 d. $358

26. A can has a radius of 1.5 inches and a height of 3 inches. Which of the following best represents the volume of the can?

 a. 17.2 in^3
 b. 19.4 in^3
 c. 21.2 in^3
 d. 23.4 in^3

27. Ann must walk from Point A to Point B and then to Point C. Finally, she will walk back to Point A. If each unit represents 5 miles, which of the following BEST represents the total distance she will have walked?

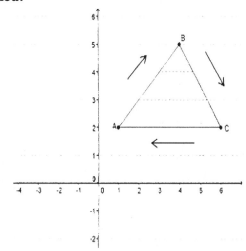

 a. 42 miles
 b. 48 miles
 c. 56 miles
 d. 64 miles

28. When a teacher explains that the order of the addends or factors does not affect the sum or product, he is teaching a lesson about:

 a. Comparing and ordering fractions
 b. The properties of real numbers
 c. Using ratios and proportions
 d. Inductive reasoning

29. A dartboard consists of two concentric circles with radii of 3 inches and 6 inches. If a dart is thrown onto the board, what is the probability the dart will land in the inner circle?

    a. $\frac{1}{4}$

    b. $\frac{1}{2}$

    c. $\frac{1}{3}$

    d. $\frac{1}{5}$

30. An equation of a hyperbola has the form:

    a. $y = ax$
    b. $y = ax^2 + b$
    c. $x^2 - y^2 = a$
    d. $x^2 + y^2 = a$

31. Which of the following is most important for a second-grade teacher to consider when evaluating a student's math ability on the basis of standardized test results?

    a. Standardized tests have proved to be consistently reliable in gauging students' mathematical abilities.
    b. Standardized tests have proved to be consistently unreliable in gauging students' mathematical abilities.
    c. Children of primary school age change rapidly and may test differently from one day to another.
    d. Standardized tests are generally based on insufficient or unreliable research.

32. The best time to introduce a student to subtraction with two-digit numerals is:

    a. Before the student reaches the fourth grade
    b. When the student has proved proficient in adding long columns of numbers
    c. When the student has achieved automatic response to subtraction facts
    d. When the student expresses an interest in advancing his or her subtraction skills

33. Given the sequence $[(0, 3), (1, 6), (2, 9), \dots, (7, x)]$, what is the value of x?

    a. 12
    b. 15
    c. 18
    d. 24

34. A fifth-grade teacher assigns her students a new math problem to be solved by the end of the day. Which of these is the most effective method of assessing students' work?

    a. Administering a standardized test
    b. Classroom observation
    c. Portfolio assessment
    d. Small group discussion

35. Which of these is true of all quadrilaterals?

    a. The opposite sides are parallel
    b. The opposite sides are of equal length
    c. The sum of the measures of the interior angles is 360 degrees
    d. The opposite angles are equal in measure

36. What is 25% of 160?

    a. 32
    b. 40
    c. 44
    d. 64

37. Given the following statements, which conclusion is logically valid?

       If Tom is a good teacher, then Tom cares about his students.
       Tom does not care about his students.

    a. Tom is a good teacher
    b. Tom is not a good teacher
    c. Tom may or may not be a good teacher
    d. Not all good teachers care about their students

38. The equation $4(7 + 5) = 4 \times 7 + 4 \times 5$ demonstrate the:

    a. Distributive property of multiplication over addition
    b. Commutative property of multiplication
    c. Associative property of multiplication
    d. Inverse property of multiplication

39. Ride Service A charges a flat rate of $10 for the first 10 miles, plus 25 cents per mile for anything over 10 miles. Ride Service B charges 40 cents per mile. Both services charge the same for a trip that is how long?

    a. 40 miles
    b. 45 miles
    c. 50 miles
    d. 55 miles

40. In a class of 24 students, 18 completed their projects on time. What fraction of the students failed to complete their projects on time?

    a. 1/4
    b. 2/3
    c. 3/4
    d. 5/8

Science

41. The part of the human excretory system most responsible for maintaining normal body temperature is the:

    a. kidney.
    b. bladder.
    c. liver.
    d. sweat glands.

42. A teacher tells the class about a new drug that is being tested on 200 volunteer subjects. Half the volunteers are given the new drug while the other half are given a harmless sugar pill. The volunteers who are given the sugar pill serve as the:

    a. Control group
    b. Experimental group
    c. Variable
    d. Indicator

43. Which of the following is a quantitative property?

    a. Texture
    b. Luster
    c. Density
    d. Scent

44. Which type of simple machine is this seesaw?

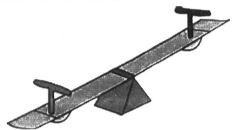

    a. Inclined plane
    b. Lever
    c. Wedge
    d. Wheel and axle

45. A horse is an example of a(n) _____.

    a. omnivore
    b. carnivore
    c. decomposer
    d. herbivore

46. Which of the following is true about how light is absorbed?

    a. The sky is blue because the atmosphere reflects only blue wavelengths.
    b. The sky is blue because the atmosphere absorbs only blue wavelengths.
    c. Glass is transparent to all of the frequencies of light within the spectrum.
    d. Wood, metal, and other opaque materials reflect all wavelengths of light.

47. Which of the following statements is NOT true?

a. The Earth rotates on its axis once every 24 hours
b. A solar eclipse can only occur during a new moon
c. The Moon rotates on its axis as it revolves around the Earth
d. A lunar eclipse occurs when the Moon passes between the Earth and the Sun

48. An important difference between plant cells and animal cells is that:

a. Only animal cells have nuclei
b. Only animal cells have mitochondria
c. Only plant cells have organelles
d. Only plant cells have rigid cellulose walls

49. What does a food chain show?

a. The flow of energy between organisms
b. Very type of species living in a habitat
c. The population of each species in a habitat
d. The number of offspring a species will produce in a year

50. Lions live in savannah and grassland regions where there are tall dry grasses. Lions must sneak up and stalk their prey. What is the most likely reason for a lion's sand colored coat?

a. It allows lions to hide within the grass
b. The light color of their coat reflects heat from the Sun
c. A lion's coloring helps it attract mates
d. It allows them to run faster than their prey

51. Which action will help dissolve a gas in a liquid if the gas and liquid are placed in a sealed container?

a. Heat the liquid.
b. Cool the liquid.
c. Shake the container.
d. Decrease the pressure on the lid.

52. What is the definition of work?

a. The amount of energy used to accomplish a job
b. The force used to move a mass over a distance
c. The amount of power per unit of time
d. Energy stored in an object due to its position
e. Force multiplied by the time over which the force acts

53. The principal cause of acid precipitation is:

a. Nuclear power production
b. Soil erosion
c. The burning of coal and petroleum products
d. Water pollution

54. Remoras are fish that attach themselves to sharks and feed on the food particles left over by the larger fish. The shark is neither harmed nor helped by the remora's actions. This type of symbiotic relationship is best described as:
a. Parasitism
b. Commensalism
c. Mutualism
d. Passive transport

55. Botanists, zoologists, physiologists, and ecologists are all specialists in the field of:
a. Chemistry
b. Biology
c. Physics
d. Social science

56. Which of the following statements about the Moon is NOT true?
a. Only one side of the Moon is seen from Earth.
b. The Moon only rotates once in one orbit around the Earth.
c. The Moon is slowly moving closer to the Earth.
d. The gravitational acceleration on the surface of the Moon is approximately one-sixth of the gravitational acceleration on the surface of the Earth.

57. A pulley lifts a 10-kg object 10 m into the air in 5 minutes. Using this information, you can calculate which of the following?
a. Mechanical advantage
b. Efficiency
c. Frictional resistance
d. Power

58. A spoon that is placed in a bowl of hot soup becomes warm as a result of:
a. Convection
b. Conduction
c. Radiation
d. Advection

59. In relation to the water cycle, which of the following statements concerning transpiration is NOT true?
a. As relative humidity increases, the rate of transpiration increases.
b. As winds increase, the rate of transpiration increases.
c. As temperatures increase, the rate of transpiration increases.
d. As soil moisture decreases, the rate of transpiration decreases.

60. Rocks are classified as *igneous*, *metamorphic*, or *sedimentary* based on:
a. How they were formed
b. Their texture
c. The minerals they contain
d. Their age

61. What are pure substances that consist of more than one type of atom?

a. Elements
b. Compounds
c. Molecules
d. Mixtures

62. A teacher takes her class on a walk through the woods to study local flora and fauna. This activity is likely to appeal most to students who favor which learning style?

a. Visual
b. Auditory
c. Tactile
d. Kinesthetic

63. On a trip to the planetarium, the class views a chunk of rock that has fallen from the sky and landed on Earth. The object they are looking at is a:

a. Comet
b. Meteor
c. Meteoroid
d. Meteorite

64. Heat is transmitted through solid materials via:

a. Conduction
b. Convection
c. Radiation
d. All three

65. Prokaryotic and eukaryotic cells are similar in having which of the following?

a. Membrane-bound organelles
b. Protein-studded DNA
c. Presence of a nucleus
d. Integral membrane proteins in the plasma membrane
e. Flagella composed of microtubules

66. Which of the following best describes Earth's atmosphere?

a. 25% nitrogen, 55% oxygen, 20% water vapor and other gases
b. 78% nitrogen, 21% oxygen, 1% water vapor and other gases
c. 38% nitrogen, 60% oxygen, 2% water vapor and other gases
d. 90% nitrogen, 5% oxygen, 5% water vapor and other gases

67. The atomic number of an element is determined by:

a. The number of neutrons in the nucleus of an atom
b. The number of protons in the nucleus of an atom
c. The number of protons plus the number of neutrons in an atom
d. The number of protons plus the number of electrons in an atom

68. Which of the following is NOT characteristic of scientific inquiry?
a. Continual posing of questions and testing of hypotheses
b. Objective analysis of experimental data
c. Ongoing peer review of shared information
d. The assumption that published literature is accurate and unbiased

69. Chemistry students are always told to add acid to water rather than adding water to acid. The reason for this is that:
a. Students need to learn to follow directions precisely to ensure accurate results
b. Adding water to acid can cause the acid to boil violently
c. Adding acid to water tends to slow down the chemical reaction
d. Adding water to acid produces toxic gases

70. The layer of Earth's atmosphere that is closest to our planet is the:
a. Troposphere
b. Ionosphere
c. Stratosphere
d. Mesosphere

71. A student is working on a science project and is going through each step of the scientific method. After the student conducts his or her first experiment and records the results of the experimental test, what should the student do next?
a. Communicate the results.
b. Draw a conclusion.
c. Repeat the experiment.
d. Create a hypothesis.

72. The condition of balance and dynamic stability that characterizes living systems under normal conditions is called:
a. Homeostasis
b. Metabolism
c. Respiration
d. Symbiosis

73. All of the following are true regarding wind energy, EXCEPT:
a. Wind turbines use space inefficiently, but they have low operational costs.
b. Wind is not a reliable source of energy in all geographic locations.
c. Wind turbines are expensive to manufacture and install.
d. Wind turbines are a threat to wildlife.

74. Which of the following is NOT generally true regarding solubility?
a. Increasing temperature increases the solubility of a solid in a liquid.
b. Increasing temperature increases the solubility of a gas in a liquid.
c. Increasing the pressure has little effect on the solubility of a solid in a liquid.
d. Increasing partial pressure of a gas decreases the solubility of a gas in a liquid.

75. The density of helium is much lower than that of air. How does the speed of sound traveling through helium gas compare to the speed of sound in air?

    a. It is faster.
    b. It is slower.
    c. It is the same speed.
    d. It cannot be determined without knowing their atomic masses.

76. Which of the following elements do plants NOT need in order to undergo photosynthesis?

    a. Carbon
    b. Oxygen
    c. Nitrogen
    d. Hydrogen

77. Which part of a hurricane features the strongest winds and greatest rainfall?

    a. Eye wall
    b. Front
    c. Eye
    d. Outward spiral

78. The first step in conducting a scientific investigation is to:

    a. Formulate a hypothesis
    b. Perform an experiment
    c. Analyze all available data
    d. State the problem to be solved

79. Which of the following creates an electromagnet?

    a. Rapidly spinning and rotating electrons inside an iron bar
    b. An iron bar moving inside a coil of wire that contains a current
    c. The movement of electrons through a complete circuit
    d. Convection currents within the liquid core of Earth's interior
    e. Translational and vibrational motion of atoms

80. How are igneous rocks formed?

    a. Years of sediment are laid down on top of each other and forced together.
    b. Acid rain caused by pollution creates holes in metamorphic rocks.
    c. Dust and pebbles are pressed together underground from Earth's heat and pressure.
    d. Magma from a volcanic eruption cools and hardens.

Answer Key and Explanations

Mathematics

1. D: Students need to learn and practice computation skills, but they also need to learn that the mathematical skills they acquire in the classroom have practical value in their lives outside of school.

2. D: For the Final, the third quartile is 87. Since 75% of the data in a set is below the third quartile, there is a 75% chance, or a probability of 0.75, that a test score chosen at random from the Final scored below 87.

3. C: Choice C is the absolute value function. A function is a relationship in which for every element of the domain (x), there is exactly one element of the range (y). Graphically, a relationship between x and y can be identified as a function if the graph passes the vertical line test.

The first relation is a parabola on its side, which fails the vertical line test for functions. Choice B also fails the vertical line test and is therefore not a function. The relation in Choice D pairs two elements of the range with one of the elements of the domain, so it is also not a function.

4. A: A triangular pyramid has four triangular faces. The arrangement of these faces in a two-dimensional figure is a net of a triangular pyramid if the figure can be folded to form a triangular pyramid. Choice B represents a rectangular pyramid, choice C is a triangular prism, and choice D is a square pyramid.

5. D: Each student is a unique individual, and different students may have different ways of conceptualizing the same problem. In the long run, allowing students to find their own ways of thinking about mathematics will make them better problem solvers. Mental math has an important role to play in everyday life. Memorization and drills also have their place, but they should not be the central focus in the classroom.

6. C: Each coin has an equal probability of coming up heads or tails, so the probability of tails for each coin is ½. For two coins, the probability is ½ × ½, or 1 in 4.

7. B: 48/120 of the students failed. 48/120 = 0.40, or 40%.

8. C: The theoretical probability is $\frac{1}{2}$, and $\frac{1}{2}(300) = 150$.

9. D: The area of a parallelogram is equal to Base × Height. The height cannot be determined just by measuring the length of the four sides. More information is required.

10. B: When the dress is marked down by 20%, the cost of the dress is 80% of its original price. Since a percentage can be written as a fraction by placing the percentage over 100, the reduced price of the dress can be written as $\frac{80}{100}x$, or $\frac{4}{5}x$, where x is the original price. When discounted an extra 25%, the dress costs 75% of the reduced price. This results in the expression $\frac{75}{100}\left(\frac{4}{5}x\right)$, which can be simplified to $\frac{3}{4}\left(\frac{4}{5}x\right)$, or $\frac{3}{5}x$. So the final price of the dress is three-fifths of the original price.

11. D: When a figure is reflected twice over non-parallel lines, the resulting transformation is a rotation about the point of intersection of the two lines of reflection. The two lines of reflection

121

$y = x - 3$ and $x = 0$ intersect at $(0, -3)$. So, $\Delta A''B''C''$ represents a rotation of ΔABC about the point $(0, -3)$. The angle of rotation is equal to twice the angle between the two lines of reflection when measured in a clockwise direction from the first to the second line of reflection. Since the angle between the lines or reflection measures 135°, the angle of rotation which is the composition of the two reflections measures 270°.

12. C: The amount he donates is equal to $0.01 \times (\$45,000)$. Thus, he donates \$450.

13. C: The relationship between Kate and her shadow is the same as the relationship between Sara and her shadow, which means the following proportion can be created.

$$\frac{\text{Kate's Height}}{\text{Kate's Shadow}} = \frac{\text{Sara's Height}}{\text{Sara's Shadow}}$$

If Sara's shadow is 16 inches longer than Kate's, it is 48 inches long.

$$\frac{40}{32} = \frac{x}{38}$$
$$32x = 48 \times 40$$
$$32x = 1,920$$
$$x = \frac{1,920}{32}$$
$$x = 60$$

Therefore, Sara is 60 inches tall.

14. D: If the distance between the two houses is 10 cm on the map, then the actual distance between the houses is 100 m. To find x, use the Pythagorean theorem:

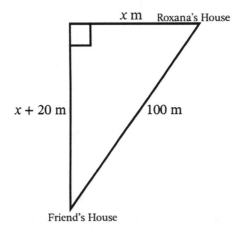

$$x^2 + (x + 20)^2 = (100)^2$$
$$x^2 + x^2 + 40x + 400 = 10,000$$
$$2x^2 + 40x - 9,600 = 0$$
$$2(x^2 + 20x - 4,800) = 0$$
$$2(x - 60)(x + 80) = 0$$
$$x = 60 \quad x = -80$$

Since x represents a distance, it cannot equal –80. Since $x = 60$, $x + 20 = 80$. Roxana walks a total of 140 m to get to her friend's house.

15. C. The original price may be modeled by the equation:

$$(x - 0.45x) + 0.0875(x - 0.45x) = \$39.95$$

This simplifies to $0.598125x = \$39.95$. Dividing each side of the equation by the coefficient of x gives $x \approx \$66.79$.

16. C: A system of linear equations can be solved by using matrices or by using the graphing, substitution, or elimination (also called linear combination) method. The elimination method is shown here:

$$3x + 4y = 2$$
$$2x + 6y = -2$$

In order to eliminate x by linear combination, multiply the top equation by 2 and the bottom equation by –3 so that the coefficients of the x-terms will be additive inverses.

$$2(3x + 4y = 2)$$
$$-3(2x + 6y = -2)$$

Then, add the two equations and solve for y.

$$6x + 8y = 4$$
$$\underline{-6x - 18y = 6}$$
$$-10y = 10$$
$$y = -1$$

Substitute –1 for y in either of the given equations and solve for x.

$$3x + 4y = 2$$
$$3x + 4(-1) = 2$$
$$3x - 4 = 2$$
$$3x = 6$$
$$x = 2$$

The solution to the system of equations is $(2, -1)$.

17. C: The student needs to determine what she is being asked to find out before she can decide what equations or steps are needed to solve the problem. Comparing the problem to others like it may be useful, but it is not the first step in solving the problem.

18. B: When you have a ratio, you can find the fraction that each part of the ratio is of the whole by putting it over the sum of the parts. In other words, since the ratio of wages and benefits to other costs is $2 : 3$, the amount of money spent on wages and benefits is $\frac{2}{2+3} = \frac{2}{5}$ of total expenditures.

$$\frac{2}{5} \times \$130,000 = \$52,000$$

Therefore, the company spends $52,000 on wages and benefits each month.

19. B: Similar figures have the same shape but not necessarily the same size.

20. D: Levi walked 3 miles from home and then back again, so he walked a total of 6 miles. Therefore, statement III is true. He traveled these 6 miles in 6 hours, so his average speed was 1 mph. Therefore, statement I is true. He walked 3 miles from point A to B in 1 hour and 2 miles from E to F in 1 hour, so his speed averaged 3 mph between A and B and 2 mph between E and F. Therefore, statement II is false.

21. B: The formula states that Part = Percent × Whole. Sixty percent equals .60, or 60/100, which can be reduced to 3/5. Thus the correct answer is $\frac{3}{5} \times 720$.

22. C: The graph shown is the exponential function $y = 2^x$. Notice that the graph passes through $(-2, 0.25)$, $(0,1)$, and $(2,4)$. A quick check of each option demonstrates the fit:

x	x^2	$\sqrt{x}$	2^x	$\log_2 x$
-2	4	undefined in $\mathbb{R}$	0.25	undefined
0	0	0	1	undefined
2	4	$\sqrt{2}$	4	1

23. D: The chance of picking one of the four aces from a deck of 52 cards is $\frac{4}{52}$. After the first ace has been picked, the chance of picking one of the three remaining aces from the remaining 51 cards in the deck is $\frac{3}{51}$. The chances of both events occurring is $\frac{4}{52} \times \frac{3}{51}$ which equals $\frac{12}{2652}$ or $\frac{1}{221}$.

24. C: The range is the spread of the data. It can be calculated for each subject by subtracting the lowest test score from the highest, or it can be determined visually from the graph. The difference between the highest and lowest test scores in History is $98 - 72 = 26$ points. The range for each of the other subjects is greater.

25. B: If there is an even number of values, the median is the mean, or arithmetic average, of the two middle values. $\$88 + \$94 = \$182$. $\$182 \div 2 = \$91$. If the problem had asked for the mean of the four values, choice A would have been correct.

26. C: The volume of a cylinder may be calculated using the formula $V = \pi r^2 h$, where r represents the radius and h represents the height. Substituting 1.5 for r and 3 for h gives $V = \pi (1.5)^2 (3)$, which simplifies to $V \approx 21.2$.

27. D: The perimeter of the triangle is equal to the sum of the side lengths. The length of the longer diagonal side may be represented as $d = \sqrt{(4-1)^2 + (5-2)^2}$, which simplifies to $d = \sqrt{18}$. The length of the shorter diagonal side may be represented as $d = \sqrt{(6-4)^2 + (2-5)^2}$, which simplifies to $d = \sqrt{13}$. The base length is 5 units. Thus, the perimeter is equal to $5 + \sqrt{18} + \sqrt{13}$, which is approximately 12.85 units. Since each unit represents 5 miles, the total distance she will have walked is equal to the product of 12.85 and 5, or approximately 64 miles.

28. B: The teacher has explained the commutative property, which is one of the properties of real numbers.

29. A: The probability that the dart will land in the inner circle is equal to the ratio of the area of inner circle to the area of the outer circle, or $\frac{\pi(3)^2}{\pi(6)^2}$. This reduces to $\frac{1}{4}$.

30. C: The first formula describes a straight line that passes through the origin at (0,0), the second describes a parabola with y-intercept at b, and the fourth describes a circle centered on the origin with radius $\sqrt{a}$.

31. C: Children in the primary grades are in a rapid stage of development, and their test score on any individual test on a given day may not be a reliable indication of their mathematical skills. This is not to suggest that standardized tests are based on inadequate research or that their results are not a valid reflection of the test-taker's level of skill on the day the test was taken.

32. C: A student is not ready to solve more complex subtraction problems until he or she has mastered all the single-digit subtraction facts. Grade level, proficiency in addition, and the desire to move ahead are not sufficient indications of the student's readiness.

33. D: $(7, x)$ represents the eighth point in this sequence. Thus, the corresponding x value equals 3×8, or 24.

34. C: Students should submit written samples of their work for the teacher to review on a daily basis. Standardized tests would not be appropriate for assessing the student's understanding of the given task. As students are likely to work on the problems at different times, classroom observation would not be practical, and group discussions would not necessarily be useful for assessment purposes.

35. C: The interior angles of any quadrilateral add up to 360 degrees. The other choices are only true of certain quadrilaterals.

36. B: To solve, first convert 25% to a decimal: 0.25. Then, multiply 160 by 0.25 to get 40.

37. B: Let p = 'Tom is a good teacher.' Let q = 'Tom cares about his students.' The given statement says: If p, then q. The contrapositive, which is also true, says: If not q, then not p. Thus, if Tom does not care about his students, Tom is not a good teacher.

38. A: The distributive property states that $a(b + c) = a \times b + b \times c$. The cumulative property allows real numbers to be added or multiplied in any order. The associative property states that the order in which real numbers are added or multiplied together makes no difference. The inverse property states that every real number has a multiplicative inverse, or reciprocal, such that $n \times \frac{1}{n} = 1$.

39. C: The expression representing the charge for Ride Service A is $\$10 + \$0.25(m - 10)$, where m is the number of miles traveled. Set this expression equal to the charge for Ride Service B, which is $\$0.40m$. Solve for m to find the number of miles for which the two companies charge the same amount.

$$\$10 + \$0.25(m - 10) = \$0.40m$$
$$\$10 + \$0.25m - \$2.5 = \$0.40m$$
$$\$7.50 + \$0.25m = \$0.40m$$
$$\$7.50 = \$0.15m$$
$$m = 50$$

So, the cost of the two services would be the same for a 50-mile ride.

40. A: If 18 of 24 students completed their projects, then 6 of 24 failed to do so. $\frac{6}{24} = \frac{1}{4}$.

Science

41. D: Blood is cooled as it passes through capillaries surrounding the sweat glands. Heat is absorbed along with excess salt and water and transferred to the glands as sweat. Droplets of sweat then evaporate from the skin surface to dissipate heat and cool the body. The kidney, bladder, and liver are not involved in regulating body temperature.

42. A: The control in an experiment is not subject to the variable being tested—in this case, the new drug. The volunteers who are given the drug comprise the experimental group.

43. C: Quantitative properties are characteristics that can be objectively measured. Density is measured using units of mass and volume, making it a quantitative property. Texture (A) is related to the way a surface looks or feels, luster (B) refers to how reflective a surface is, and scent (D) is the way something smells. Texture, luster, and scent cannot be measured and are not expressed using numerical values, so they are qualitative properties, not quantitative properties.

44. B: Lever. A seesaw is a flat board that pivots on a fulcrum, meaning that a seesaw is a lever. Therefore, the correct choice is B.

45. D: Horses eat plants but do not eat meat, so they are herbivores. Omnivores (A) eat plants and meat, while carnivores (B) eat meat but do not eat plants. Decomposers (C) consume only dead plants and animals, as they break down remains as a source of energy.

46. A: The reason the sky looks blue to us is because the earth's atmosphere absorbs the wavelengths of all colors of light in the spectrum except for the wavelengths of the color blue, which it reflects back so that we see it. Therefore (B) is incorrect. Glass appears transparent to us; however, it is really only transparent to the light frequencies (wavelengths) that we can see, but to ultraviolet light frequencies, which we cannot see, glass is actually opaque. Wood, metal, and other materials look opaque to us *not* because they reflect light (D), but rather because they absorb light.

47. D: A lunar eclipse occurs when the full moon moves through the Earth's shadow. A solar eclipse occurs when a new moon passes between the Earth and the Sun.

48. D: Cellulose is a structural carbohydrate that protects and supports plant cells. Nuclei, mitochondria, and organelles are found in both plant and animal cells.

49. A: A food chain shows how energy flows from one consumer to another. The arrows point in the direction that energy moves. For example, if an arrow points from a flower to a bee, then the energy from the flower flows to the bee as the bee eats the nectar of the flower.

50. A: Lions live in a wide open area where there are few large objects to hide behind. In order to get close enough to their prey to chase and attack it, they must be able to sneak up on it. Their coloration is similar to the color of the tall grasses where they live. This allows the lions to blend into their surroundings and get close to their prey.

51. B: If a gas and a liquid are placed in a sealed container, cooling the liquid will help dissolve the gas into the liquid. Gases have higher solubility in liquids at lower temperatures. At higher temperatures, the gas molecules will have more kinetic energy and will have enough energy to overcome intermolecular interactions with the liquid solvent and leave the solution. This also explains why heating the liquid is incorrect. Shaking the container is also incorrect as this would give the gas energy to escape. Decreasing the pressure on the lid may or may not significantly affect the pressure inside the vessel depending on the nature of the vessel, but decreasing the pressure inside the vessel would decrease the solubility of the gas in the liquid.

52. B: Work is defined as the force used to move a mass over a distance. Choice A may be a secular (non-scientific) definition of work. Choice C is the definition of power. Choice D is the definition of potential energy. Choice E is the definition of impulse.

53. C: Acid rain results from the release of nitrogen and sulfur oxides into the atmosphere. The generation of electricity, especially by coal power plants and gasoline-powered motor vehicles, are the main sources of these destructive pollutants. Although the production of nuclear power may carry other risks, it does not contribute to the problem of acid precipitation.

54. B: Commensalism is a relationship between two organisms in which one organism is benefited and the other is neither harmed nor helped. Parasitism is a relationship in which one organism benefits but the other is harmed. Mutualism is a relationship in which both organisms benefit. Passive transport is a process such as osmosis by which materials are absorbed into cells.

55. B: Biologists examine the structure, function, growth, origin, and classification of living organisms. Botanists specialize in the study of plant life; zoologists specialize in animal species; physiologists focus on mechanical, physical, and biochemical functions of organisms; and ecologists study the relationship between living things and their environment. Physicists study the interaction of matter and energy in the physical world while chemists focus on the chemical structure of matter. Social scientists, including anthropologists, economists, and psychologists focus on human behavior and social interactions.

56. C: The Moon is slowly moving further away from the Earth. The Moon is moving a little less than 4 cm a year away from the Earth. Since the Moon only rotates once in every orbit around the Earth, the same side is always seen from Earth. The acceleration of gravity on the surface of the Moon is approximately one-sixth of the gravitational acceleration on the surface of the Earth. Although the Moon has less than 1/80 the mass of the Earth, it also has a smaller radius, and the acceleration of gravity on the surface depends on both.

57. D: The equation for power, $power = \frac{work}{time}$, can be utilized. The mass of the object (10 kg) and the distance (10 m) can be used to calculate work, $work = mass \times (gravitational\ acceleration) \times distance$. The value for time is provided.

58. B: Conduction is the transfer and distribution of heat energy from one molecule to the next within a substance. The spoon becomes warmer because the heat from the soup is conducted along the spoon. Convection is the transfer of heat energy in a gas or liquid through the movement of currents. Radiation is the transfer of heat through empty space in the form of rays or waves. Advection is the transfer of heat or other atmospheric properties by the horizontal movement of air.

59. A: As the relative humidity in the area surrounding a plant increases, the rate of transpiration decreases. It is more difficult for water to evaporate into the more saturated air. As the relative humidity decreases, the rate of transpiration increases.

60. A: Igneous rocks form from the solidification of molten rock; metamorphic rocks form from changes in heat, pressure, or chemical activity; and sedimentary rocks are formed mainly by the compaction of rock fragments and other materials. All three types of rock may vary in texture, age, and mineral content.

61. B: Elements and compounds are both pure substances. Elements consist of only one type of atom. Compounds consist of more than one type of atom. Molecules may make up either elements or compounds. Mixtures are two or more substances that are physically combined but not chemically united.

62. D: Kinesthetic learners are most receptive to new information when they can use body movement to explore the world around them. Like tactile learners, they profit most from a hands-on approach to education. Visual learners learn best when they are shown pictures or written materials, while auditory learners absorb information most effectively when it is presented verbally.

63. D: A meteoroid is an object smaller than an asteroid that revolves around any interplanetary body. The visible path of a meteoroid as it crosses the sky is called a meteor or, more commonly, a shooting star. A meteoroid that reaches the surface of the Earth without being completely vaporized is called a meteorite. A comet is a small chunk of matter that orbits the sun in an elliptical path, and is often composed of ice.

64. A: Three ways of transmitting heat are conduction (A), convection (B), and radiation (C). When heat is transmitted through solids, this is done via conduction. Conduction occurs between solid materials directly contacting one another. Convection (B) is how heat travels through liquids and gases. Heat makes them expand, lowering their density so they rise. When they cool, they recover density and fall. This heating-rising and cooling-falling process creates a current known as convection. Radiation (C), like the heat from the sun, occurs when electromagnetic waves travel through space and transfer heat to objects, like the Earth, that they touch. Therefore, (D) is incorrect.

65. D: Both prokaryotes and eukaryotes interact with the extracellular environment and use membrane-bound or membrane-associated proteins to achieve this. They both use diffusion and active transport to move materials in and out of their cells. Prokaryotes have very few proteins associated with their DNA, whereas eukaryotes' DNA is richly studded with proteins. Both types of living things can have flagella, although with different structural characteristics in the two groups. The most important differences between prokaryotes and eukaryotes are the lack of a nucleus and membrane-bound organelles in prokaryotes.

66. B: The abundant nitrogen in Earth's atmosphere is left over from the time billions of years ago when volcanoes hurled it into the air. Nitrogen tends to be unreactive and does not readily bond with other elements. Oxygen and hydrogen bond together to make the water that covers much of our planet's surface.

67. B: The atomic number is equal to the number of protons in the nucleus, which is equal to the number of electrons. The number of protons plus the number of neutrons is equal to the mass number of the atom.

68. D: Not all scientific literature is reliable. Students must learn to distinguish between sources that are consistent with experimental evidence and those that are biased or misleading in their conclusions. Scientists study one another's work to direct and support original research, but they recognize that interpretations of data may vary and that existing theories are always subject to testing and revision.

69. B: The combination of water and acid is exothermic. The addition of water to acid results in a solution that is initially highly concentrated, and enough heat may be produced to cause the acid to boil and splash out of the container.

70. A: The troposphere contains three-quarters of the atmosphere's mass and almost all of its water vapor. It is followed by the stratosphere, which is separated from the outermost ionosphere by the mesosphere.

71. C: Repeating the experiment validates data. Each separate experiment is called a repetition. It should be possible to replicate the results of experiments or tests. Similar data gathered from many experiments can also be used to quantify the validity of the hypothesis. Repeating the experiments allows the student to observe variation in the results. Variation in data can be caused by a variety of errors or may be evidence against the hypothesis. Answer D, create a hypothesis, comes before experiments. Answer A, communicate the results, and B, draw a conclusion, occur after testing.

72. A: Homeostasis is the process whereby an organism maintains the constant internal conditions necessary for life. Dynamic equilibrium must be maintained even as external conditions continually change. Metabolism refers to the combined chemical processes within a living cell or organism that are necessary for maintaining life. Respiration refers to the process by which cells derive energy from organic molecules. Symbiosis refers to a close association of two dissimilar species that is usually beneficial to one or both of the organisms.

73. A: Pros of wind energy include space efficiency, no pollution, and low operational costs. Cons of wind energy include wind fluctuation, threats to wildlife, and the expense to manufacture and install.

74. B: Solubility is the amount of solute present in saturated solution. For a gas solute in a liquid solvent, increasing the temperature increases the kinetic energy of the gas molecules, which decreases the solubility of the gas in the liquid. Increasing the pressure of the gas increases the number of particles escaping from the surface and decreases the solubility. For a solid solute in a liquid solvent, increasing the temperature increases the kinetic energy, which increases the number of collisions and increases the solubility. Increasing the pressure of a solid solute in a liquid has little or no effect on solubility.

75. A: Sound travels much faster through helium than through air. Generally, the speed of sound can be calculated by $v = \sqrt{k \times \frac{P}{\rho}}$, where k is the heat capacity ratio for the gas (the heat capacity at constant pressure divided by the heat capacity at constant volume), P is pressure, and ρ is density. Since helium has a much lower density, it would have a higher speed.

76. C: Plants do not require nitrogen for photosynthesis. Plants need access sunlight, carbon dioxide, and water to undergo photosynthesis. Carbon dioxide contains carbon (A) and oxygen (B), and water contains hydrogen (D) and oxygen (B).

77. A: The eye wall of a hurricane has the strongest winds and the greatest rainfall. The eye wall is the tower-like rim of the eye. It is from this wall that clouds extend out, which are seen from above as the classic outward spiral pattern. A hurricane front is the outermost edge of its influence; although there will be heavy winds and rain in this area, the intensity will be relatively small. The eye of a hurricane is actually a place of surprising peace. In this area, dry and cool air rushes down to the ground or sea. Once there, the air is caught up in the winds of the eye wall and is driven outward at a furious pace.

78. D: If the question to be answered is not clearly stated at the outset, time and resources may be wasted in studying irrelevant data. Once the problem to be solved has been determined, a hypothesis can be formulated and an experiment can be designed to test it.

79. B: An iron bar moving inside a coil of wire that contains a current would create an electromagnet. Choice A creates a magnetic field. Choice C creates an electric current. Choice D creates the Earth's magnetic field. Choice E creates thermal energy.

80. D: Igneous rocks are formed when magma in the Earth erupts through cracks in the crust. There, the lava cools, creating a hard structure with many air pockets or holes.

How to Overcome Test Anxiety

Just the thought of taking a test is enough to make most people a little nervous. A test is an important event that can have a long-term impact on your future, so it's important to take it seriously and it's natural to feel anxious about performing well. But just because anxiety is normal, that doesn't mean that it's helpful in test taking, or that you should simply accept it as part of your life. Anxiety can have a variety of effects. These effects can be mild, like making you feel slightly nervous, or severe, like blocking your ability to focus or remember even a simple detail.

If you experience test anxiety—whether severe or mild—it's important to know how to beat it. To discover this, first you need to understand what causes test anxiety.

Causes of Test Anxiety

While we often think of anxiety as an uncontrollable emotional state, it can actually be caused by simple, practical things. One of the most common causes of test anxiety is that a person does not feel adequately prepared for their test. This feeling can be the result of many different issues such as poor study habits or lack of organization, but the most common culprit is time management. Starting to study too late, failing to organize your study time to cover all of the material, or being distracted while you study will mean that you're not well prepared for the test. This may lead to cramming the night before, which will cause you to be physically and mentally exhausted for the test. Poor time management also contributes to feelings of stress, fear, and hopelessness as you realize you are not well prepared but don't know what to do about it.

Other times, test anxiety is not related to your preparation for the test but comes from unresolved fear. This may be a past failure on a test, or poor performance on tests in general. It may come from comparing yourself to others who seem to be performing better or from the stress of living up to expectations. Anxiety may be driven by fears of the future—how failure on this test would affect your educational and career goals. These fears are often completely irrational, but they can still negatively impact your test performance.

Elements of Test Anxiety

As mentioned earlier, test anxiety is considered to be an emotional state, but it has physical and mental components as well. Sometimes you may not even realize that you are suffering from test anxiety until you notice the physical symptoms. These can include trembling hands, rapid heartbeat, sweating, nausea, and tense muscles. Extreme anxiety may lead to fainting or vomiting. Obviously, any of these symptoms can have a negative impact on testing. It is important to recognize them as soon as they begin to occur so that you can address the problem before it damages your performance.

The mental components of test anxiety include trouble focusing and inability to remember learned information. During a test, your mind is on high alert, which can help you recall information and stay focused for an extended period of time. However, anxiety interferes with your mind's natural processes, causing you to blank out, even on the questions you know well. The strain of testing during anxiety makes it difficult to stay focused, especially on a test that may take several hours. Extreme anxiety can take a huge mental toll, making it difficult not only to recall test information but even to understand the test questions or pull your thoughts together.

131

Effects of Test Anxiety

Test anxiety is like a disease—if left untreated, it will get progressively worse. Anxiety leads to poor performance, and this reinforces the feelings of fear and failure, which in turn lead to poor performances on subsequent tests. It can grow from a mild nervousness to a crippling condition. If allowed to progress, test anxiety can have a big impact on your schooling, and consequently on your future.

Test anxiety can spread to other parts of your life. Anxiety on tests can become anxiety in any stressful situation, and blanking on a test can turn into panicking in a job situation. But fortunately, you don't have to let anxiety rule your testing and determine your grades. There are a number of relatively simple steps you can take to move past anxiety and function normally on a test and in the rest of life.

Physical Steps for Beating Test Anxiety

While test anxiety is a serious problem, the good news is that it can be overcome. It doesn't have to control your ability to think and remember information. While it may take time, you can begin taking steps today to beat anxiety.

Just as your first hint that you may be struggling with anxiety comes from the physical symptoms, the first step to treating it is also physical. Rest is crucial for having a clear, strong mind. If you are tired, it is much easier to give in to anxiety. But if you establish good sleep habits, your body and mind will be ready to perform optimally, without the strain of exhaustion. Additionally, sleeping well helps you to retain information better, so you're more likely to recall the answers when you see the test questions.

Getting good sleep means more than going to bed on time. It's important to allow your brain time to relax. Take study breaks from time to time so it doesn't get overworked, and don't study right before bed. Take time to rest your mind before trying to rest your body, or you may find it difficult to fall asleep.

Along with sleep, other aspects of physical health are important in preparing for a test. Good nutrition is vital for good brain function. Sugary foods and drinks may give a burst of energy but this burst is followed by a crash, both physically and emotionally. Instead, fuel your body with protein and vitamin-rich foods.

Also, drink plenty of water. Dehydration can lead to headaches and exhaustion, especially if your brain is already under stress from the rigors of the test. Particularly if your test is a long one, drink water during the breaks. And if possible, take an energy-boosting snack to eat between sections.

Along with sleep and diet, a third important part of physical health is exercise. Maintaining a steady workout schedule is helpful, but even taking 5-minute study breaks to walk can help get your blood pumping faster and clear your head. Exercise also releases endorphins, which contribute to a positive feeling and can help combat test anxiety.

When you nurture your physical health, you are also contributing to your mental health. If your body is healthy, your mind is much more likely to be healthy as well. So take time to rest, nourish your body with healthy food and water, and get moving as much as possible. Taking these physical steps will make you stronger and more able to take the mental steps necessary to overcome test anxiety.

Mental Steps for Beating Test Anxiety

Working on the mental side of test anxiety can be more challenging, but as with the physical side, there are clear steps you can take to overcome it. As mentioned earlier, test anxiety often stems from lack of preparation, so the obvious solution is to prepare for the test. Effective studying may be the most important weapon you have for beating test anxiety, but you can and should employ several other mental tools to combat fear.

First, boost your confidence by reminding yourself of past success—tests or projects that you aced. If you're putting as much effort into preparing for this test as you did for those, there's no reason you should expect to fail here. Work hard to prepare; then trust your preparation.

Second, surround yourself with encouraging people. It can be helpful to find a study group, but be sure that the people you're around will encourage a positive attitude. If you spend time with others who are anxious or cynical, this will only contribute to your own anxiety. Look for others who are motivated to study hard from a desire to succeed, not from a fear of failure.

Third, reward yourself. A test is physically and mentally tiring, even without anxiety, and it can be helpful to have something to look forward to. Plan an activity following the test, regardless of the outcome, such as going to a movie or getting ice cream.

When you are taking the test, if you find yourself beginning to feel anxious, remind yourself that you know the material. Visualize successfully completing the test. Then take a few deep, relaxing breaths and return to it. Work through the questions carefully but with confidence, knowing that you are capable of succeeding.

Developing a healthy mental approach to test taking will also aid in other areas of life. Test anxiety affects more than just the actual test—it can be damaging to your mental health and even contribute to depression. It's important to beat test anxiety before it becomes a problem for more than testing.

Study Strategy

Being prepared for the test is necessary to combat anxiety, but what does being prepared look like? You may study for hours on end and still not feel prepared. What you need is a strategy for test prep. The next few pages outline our recommended steps to help you plan out and conquer the challenge of preparation.

STEP 1: SCOPE OUT THE TEST

Learn everything you can about the format (multiple choice, essay, etc.) and what will be on the test. Gather any study materials, course outlines, or sample exams that may be available. Not only will this help you to prepare, but knowing what to expect can help to alleviate test anxiety.

STEP 2: MAP OUT THE MATERIAL

Look through the textbook or study guide and make note of how many chapters or sections it has. Then divide these over the time you have. For example, if a book has 15 chapters and you have five days to study, you need to cover three chapters each day. Even better, if you have the time, leave an extra day at the end for overall review after you have gone through the material in depth.

If time is limited, you may need to prioritize the material. Look through it and make note of which sections you think you already have a good grasp on, and which need review. While you are studying, skim quickly through the familiar sections and take more time on the challenging parts.

Write out your plan so you don't get lost as you go. Having a written plan also helps you feel more in control of the study, so anxiety is less likely to arise from feeling overwhelmed at the amount to cover.

STEP 3: GATHER YOUR TOOLS

Decide what study method works best for you. Do you prefer to highlight in the book as you study and then go back over the highlighted portions? Or do you type out notes of the important information? Or is it helpful to make flashcards that you can carry with you? Assemble the pens, index cards, highlighters, post-it notes, and any other materials you may need so you won't be distracted by getting up to find things while you study.

If you're having a hard time retaining the information or organizing your notes, experiment with different methods. For example, try color-coding by subject with colored pens, highlighters, or post-it notes. If you learn better by hearing, try recording yourself reading your notes so you can listen while in the car, working out, or simply sitting at your desk. Ask a friend to quiz you from your flashcards, or try teaching someone the material to solidify it in your mind.

STEP 4: CREATE YOUR ENVIRONMENT

It's important to avoid distractions while you study. This includes both the obvious distractions like visitors and the subtle distractions like an uncomfortable chair (or a too-comfortable couch that makes you want to fall asleep). Set up the best study environment possible: good lighting and a comfortable work area. If background music helps you focus, you may want to turn it on, but otherwise keep the room quiet. If you are using a computer to take notes, be sure you don't have any other windows open, especially applications like social media, games, or anything else that could distract you. Silence your phone and turn off notifications. Be sure to keep water close by so you stay hydrated while you study (but avoid unhealthy drinks and snacks).

Also, take into account the best time of day to study. Are you freshest first thing in the morning? Try to set aside some time then to work through the material. Is your mind clearer in the afternoon or evening? Schedule your study session then. Another method is to study at the same time of day that you will take the test, so that your brain gets used to working on the material at that time and will be ready to focus at test time.

STEP 5: STUDY!

Once you have done all the study preparation, it's time to settle into the actual studying. Sit down, take a few moments to settle your mind so you can focus, and begin to follow your study plan. Don't give in to distractions or let yourself procrastinate. This is your time to prepare so you'll be ready to fearlessly approach the test. Make the most of the time and stay focused.

Of course, you don't want to burn out. If you study too long you may find that you're not retaining the information very well. Take regular study breaks. For example, taking five minutes out of every hour to walk briskly, breathing deeply and swinging your arms, can help your mind stay fresh.

As you get to the end of each chapter or section, it's a good idea to do a quick review. Remind yourself of what you learned and work on any difficult parts. When you feel that you've mastered the material, move on to the next part. At the end of your study session, briefly skim through your notes again.

But while review is helpful, cramming last minute is NOT. If at all possible, work ahead so that you won't need to fit all your study into the last day. Cramming overloads your brain with more information than it can process and retain, and your tired mind may struggle to recall even previously learned information when it is overwhelmed with last-minute study. Also, the urgent nature of cramming and the stress placed on your brain contribute to anxiety. You'll be more likely to go to the test feeling unprepared and having trouble thinking clearly.

So don't cram, and don't stay up late before the test, even just to review your notes at a leisurely pace. Your brain needs rest more than it needs to go over the information again. In fact, plan to finish your studies by noon or early afternoon the day before the test. Give your brain the rest of the day to relax or focus on other things, and get a good night's sleep. Then you will be fresh for the test and better able to recall what you've studied.

STEP 6: TAKE A PRACTICE TEST

Many courses offer sample tests, either online or in the study materials. This is an excellent resource to check whether you have mastered the material, as well as to prepare for the test format and environment.

Check the test format ahead of time: the number of questions, the type (multiple choice, free response, etc.), and the time limit. Then create a plan for working through them. For example, if you have 30 minutes to take a 60-question test, your limit is 30 seconds per question. Spend less time on the questions you know well so that you can take more time on the difficult ones.

If you have time to take several practice tests, take the first one open book, with no time limit. Work through the questions at your own pace and make sure you fully understand them. Gradually work up to taking a test under test conditions: sit at a desk with all study materials put away and set a timer. Pace yourself to make sure you finish the test with time to spare and go back to check your answers if you have time.

After each test, check your answers. On the questions you missed, be sure you understand why you missed them. Did you misread the question (tests can use tricky wording)? Did you forget the information? Or was it something you hadn't learned? Go back and study any shaky areas that the practice tests reveal.

Taking these tests not only helps with your grade, but also aids in combating test anxiety. If you're already used to the test conditions, you're less likely to worry about it, and working through tests until you're scoring well gives you a confidence boost. Go through the practice tests until you feel comfortable, and then you can go into the test knowing that you're ready for it.

Test Tips

On test day, you should be confident, knowing that you've prepared well and are ready to answer the questions. But aside from preparation, there are several test day strategies you can employ to maximize your performance.

First, as stated before, get a good night's sleep the night before the test (and for several nights before that, if possible). Go into the test with a fresh, alert mind rather than staying up late to study.

Try not to change too much about your normal routine on the day of the test. It's important to eat a nutritious breakfast, but if you normally don't eat breakfast at all, consider eating just a protein bar. If you're a coffee drinker, go ahead and have your normal coffee. Just make sure you time it so that the caffeine doesn't wear off right in the middle of your test. Avoid sugary beverages, and drink enough water to stay hydrated but not so much that you need a restroom break 10 minutes into the test. If your test isn't first thing in the morning, consider going for a walk or doing a light workout before the test to get your blood flowing.

Allow yourself enough time to get ready, and leave for the test with plenty of time to spare so you won't have the anxiety of scrambling to arrive in time. Another reason to be early is to select a good seat. It's helpful to sit away from doors and windows, which can be distracting. Find a good seat, get out your supplies, and settle your mind before the test begins.

When the test begins, start by going over the instructions carefully, even if you already know what to expect. Make sure you avoid any careless mistakes by following the directions.

Then begin working through the questions, pacing yourself as you've practiced. If you're not sure on an answer, don't spend too much time on it, and don't let it shake your confidence. Either skip it and come back later, or eliminate as many wrong answers as possible and guess among the remaining ones. Don't dwell on these questions as you continue—put them out of your mind and focus on what lies ahead.

Be sure to read all of the answer choices, even if you're sure the first one is the right answer. Sometimes you'll find a better one if you keep reading. But don't second-guess yourself if you do immediately know the answer. Your gut instinct is usually right. Don't let test anxiety rob you of the information you know.

If you have time at the end of the test (and if the test format allows), go back and review your answers. Be cautious about changing any, since your first instinct tends to be correct, but make sure you didn't misread any of the questions or accidentally mark the wrong answer choice. Look over any you skipped and make an educated guess.

At the end, leave the test feeling confident. You've done your best, so don't waste time worrying about your performance or wishing you could change anything. Instead, celebrate the successful completion of this test. And finally, use this test to learn how to deal with anxiety even better next time.

> **Review Video: Test Anxiety**
> Visit mometrix.com/academy and enter code: 100340

Important Qualification

Not all anxiety is created equal. If your test anxiety is causing major issues in your life beyond the classroom or testing center, or if you are experiencing troubling physical symptoms related to your anxiety, it may be a sign of a serious physiological or psychological condition. If this sounds like your situation, we strongly encourage you to seek professional help.

Additional Bonus Material

Due to our efforts to try to keep this book to a manageable length, we've created a link that will give you access to all of your additional bonus material:

mometrix.com/bonus948/gacespedms